SOME MARRIAGES

in the

BURNED RECORD COUNTIES

of

VIRGINIA

Published by

VIRGINIA GENEALOGICAL SOCIETY

Special Publication No. 4

Please Direct All Correspondence and Book Orders to:

Southern Historical Press, Inc.
PO Box 1267
375 West Broad Street
Greenville, S.C. 29602

ISBN # 0-89308-266-X

Printed in the United States of America

INTRODUCTION

One who undertakes research, genealogical or historical, in records of certain areas of Virginia, is apt to find himself in agreement with Lord Chesterfield, who is reputed to have said that history is only a confused heap of facts.

Such may be said to be the condition of the records of the "burned counties" - a term perhaps more descriptive than accurate, used in reference to those counties in the eastern part of the state near Richmond, many or all of whose records have been lost, some by the great destruction of the Civil War, some in a series of court house fires, and some by other causes just as devastating.

Regrettably, for many years in some instances, there appears to have been little concern over the loss of records or little effort made to preserve those that remained. It is gratifying to know that recently, however, efforts by informed persons to develop an awareness on the part of those in authority have resulted in the implementation of a state-wide program to retrieve and preserve as many records as possible.

To one whose interest is genealogy, marriage records in particular are elusive. Thus it is indeed welcome news that this volume, another by the Projects Committee of the Virginia Genealogical Society in a planned series of volumes relating to burned counties, brings together many of the marriage records that have been sought.

This compilation represents an exhaustive search of the few original sources that are available. It does not include such sources as marriages by inference, marriages published in newspapers, marriages in family bible records, etc. It will be seen that such indirect sources might well be the basis of another volume to be published in the future.

This book is the result of the efforts of the following members who have contributed their time to this project:

Mrs. S. Wirt Yates   Mr. H.A. Elliott (deceased)
Mrs. James R. Lindsay   Mrs. L.J. Livingston
Mrs. John C. Matheny   Mr. Prentiss Price
Mrs. Thelma Willis (deceased)   Mr. Joseph F. Inman
            Mrs. Joseph F. Inman, Chairman

Mrs Earl Broaddus Short of Dinwiddie, Virginia, complied marriages for that county from the Deed Books found in the County Courthouse. Most of these are in the form of Minister's Returns, the earliest marriage date being 1818.

The Quaker [Friends] records included herein are those which have been photocopied in the Virginia State Library. Some of these marriages no doubt have appeared in published sources. However, the originals often give more genealogical information and were included to help the searcher identify the family. In some cases the witnesses were identified as "aunt", "brother", "mother", etc. The Quaker records, as complied, referred to people from Nansemond, Charles City, Hanover, and New Kent, the earliest being 1678.

Also included are two manuscript volumes of Hanover County marriages which have never been published: Rev. Charles Talley's Register and St. Martin's Parish Register. Rev. Charles Talley was a Baptist minister in the lower end of Hanover, and his marriages included persons from New Kent and King William Counties. St. Martin's Parish boundaries extended into Louisa County and no doubt some of the marriages found in this source may be Louisa County people.

The Virginia State Library has a file entitled, "Licenses, Marriage and Ordinary." This is a list of fees collected by the court clerks of various counties for ordinary licenses and marriage fees, 1771-1788. The clerk in most cases gave the name of both the bride and groom; the King and Queen County clerk only listed the groom's name. The date as shown is not necessarily the marriage date. It is the date of the clerk's list.

In 1963, the Virginia Genealogical Society published Virginia Marriages in Rev. John Cameron's Register and Bath Parish Register [one book]. This compilation included marriages from Prince George, Dinwiddie, and Nottoway Counties, and this publication should be consulted for marriages in this area.

Although Caroline County is considered a county with lost records, the county fortunately has a marriage register. Caroline County Marriages are currently being published in the Virginia Genealogical Society's Quarterly. Therefore, these marriages are not included in this publication, with the exception of about four or five which were found in the Licenses, Marriage and Ordinary file (1777) and were not in the Marriage Register which starts in 1783.

The Virginia Genealogical Society is to be commended on the aim and completion of this most valuable addition to its series of publications.

Jewell T. Clark
Archival Assistant
Virginia State Library

April 1972

Know all men by these present, that we Thomas Jefferson and Francis Eppes are held and firmly bound to our sovereign Lord the King his heirs and successors in the sum of fifty pounds current money of Virginia, to the payment of which will and truly to be made, we bind ourselves jointly and severally, our joint and several heirs, executors and administrators. In witness whereof we have hereto set our hands and seals this twenty third day of December in the year of our Lord one thousand seven hundred and seventy-one.

The condition of the above obligation is such that if there be no lawful cause to obstruct a marriage intended to be had and solemnized between the above bound Thomas Jefferson and Martha Skelton of the county of Charles City, widow, for which a license is desired, then this obligation is to be null and void; otherwise to remain in full force.

Replica of the marriage bond of
Thomas Jefferson and Martha Skelton
(Courtesy of Virginia State Library)

SOME MARRIAGES
IN THE
BURNED RECORD COUNTIES
OF
VIRGINIA

12 June 1786 - ABBOT, Benjamin and Sarah Flowers, of full age. (Buckingham County Marriage Bonds)

10 October 1836 - ABERNATHY, David and Amanda E.L.C.H. Hobbs. (Dinwiddie County, D.B. 2, p. 37, Minister's Return of Isham E. Hargrave)

20 January 1852 - ABERNATHY, James H. and Frances Perkins, by (I. E. Hargrave. (Dinwiddie County Marriage Book 1849-1867, p. 107)

3 December 1840 - ABERNATHY, Laban and Harriet Abernathy (Dinwiddie County, D.B. 3, p. 96, Minister's Return of I. E. Hargrave)

22 December 1848 - ABERNATHY, Thomas Jones and Louisa W. Parsons. (Dinwiddie County D.B. 6, p. 75, Minister's Return of James D. Parker)

18 January 1827 - ACRE, John and Miss _____ Martin. License obtained in Henrico County. (Rev. Talley's Register, p. 9)

9 February 1832 - ACREE, Thomas and Harriet Meredith, both of Hanover County (Rev. Talley's Register, p. 16)

25 February 1830 - ACREE, Nathaniel of King William County and Maria Heath of Hanover County. (Rev. Talley's Register, p. 13)

12 September 1793 - _____ and Elizabeth ADAMS of King and Queen. (Christ Church Parish Register, p. 257)

25 July 1840 - ADAMS, Francis, bachelor, and Miss Sarah Boaze. (Hanover County Miscellany)

8 November 1788 - ADAMS, John and Ann P. Rose of King and Queen County. (Christ Church Parish Register, p. 194)

12 November 1831 - ADAMS, John, Jr. and Mary Martin of New Kent. (Rev. Talley's Register, p. 16)

24 April 1832 - ADAMS, Thomas of King William County and Mildred Barker of Hanover. (Rev. Talley's Register, p. 17)

28 November 1833 - ADAMS, Thomas, Jr. and Elizabeth Withers. (Dinwiddie County, D.B. 1, p. 244, Minister's Returns of John Grammer, Jr.,)

14 August 1850 - ADAMS, William A. and Maria Ann Crump. (Dinwiddie County, Marriage Book 1849-67, p. 100, Minister's Return of W. E. Webb)

13 February 1787 - ADCOCK, John and Sally Wheeler, spinster. Sur. Thomas Pasley. (Buckingham County Marriage Bonds)

21 March 1785 - AKERS, John and Ann Jefferies, spinster, of

full age. Sur. Abner Lee. (Buckingham County Marriage Bonds)

26 September 1850 - AIKINS, Wm. J. and Eliza Crowder. (Dinwiddie County Marriage Book 1849-67, p. 105)

22 November 1832 - ALDRIDGE, James and Mary King. (Dinwiddie County D.B. 1, p. 4, Minister's Return of Isham E. Hargrave)

27 July 1825 - ALEXANDER, William and Mary Parsley, both of Hanover. (Rev. Talley's Register, p. 6)

13 February 1841 - ALLEN, Edmund W., bachelor, and Miss Eliza D. Talley. (Hanover County Miscellany)

26 January 1825 - ALLEN, Harwood and Paulini J. Hooper, both of Hanover. (Rev. Talley's Register, p. 5)

15 December 1831 - ALLEN, Reuben C. of Henrico County and Sarah Hooper of Hanover County. (Rev. Talley's Register, p. 16)

30 July 1779 - ALLEN, Richard of Dinwiddie County and Winefred Vaughan, widow. Sur. William Allen. (Amelia County Marriages, p. A-1)

1 December 1775-1 January 1778 - ALLEN, Samuel and Mary Mimms. (Buckingham County Licenses - marriage and ordinary. Date as reported by Clerk)

13 November 1817 - ALLEN, Wm. H. and Maria Major. Sur. Andrew Fore. (Charles City County Courthouse records)

28 August 1850 - ALLGOOD, Robert and Mrs. Eliza C. Nunnally. (Dinwiddie County Marriage Book 1849-1867, p. 101. Minister's Return of James D. Parker)

11 September 1834 - ALLISON, Albert G. and Mary Wright, both of Hanover. (Rev. Talley's Register, p. 21)

25 June 1846 - ALSTON, John J. and Mary M. Clark. (Dinwiddie County, D.B. 5, p. 295, Minister's Return of I. E. Hargrave)

21 October 1828 - ALVIS, Charles and Emily M. Buffin, daughter of Giles Buffin. Sur. Giles Buffin. (Charles City County Courthouse records)

31 May 1783 - AMBLER, John of Hanover County, son of Edward Ambler, deceased, and Frances Armistead, daughter of Gill Armistead, deceased. J. Ambler, guardian of John consents for him and is Surety. Wit. John Black and Wilson Miles Cary. (Marriages of Henrico County, Virginia 1680-1808 by Joyce H. Lindsay, p. 3)

19 May 1791 - AMBLER, JOHN of James City County and Lucy Marshall, sister of J. Marshall who consents. Sur. Jacquelin Ambler. (Marriages of Henrico County, Virginia 1680-1808 by Joyce H. Lindsay, p. 3)

21 October 1847 - AMMONS, Beverly W. and Jane Frances Snipes. William P. Snipes consents [no relationship stated]. Sur. William P. Snipes. (Charles City County Marriage License)

3 October 1818 - AMORY, Thomas C. of Gloucester County and

2

Isabella K. Weathers, before James C. Wiatt, a Justice of the Peace for Gloucester County. William Robins made oath that Thomas C. Amory "is not under the age of 21." (Marriages of Richmond County, Virginia, 1668-1853 by George H. S. King, p. 3)

11 June 1777 - ANDERSON, Benjamin and Frances Wily. (Hanover County Licenses, Marriage & Ordinary. Date as reported by Clerk)

10 January 1793 - ANDERSON, Francis and Frances Spencer of King and Queen County. (Christ Church Parish Register)

22 January 1851 - ANDERSON, George and Martha J. Williams, by Hosea Crowder. (Dinwiddie County Marriage Book 1849-1867, p. 106)

___ May 1704 - ANDERSON, Henry of Prince George County, Va. and Prudence Stratton. (Marriages of Henrico County, Virginia 1680-1808 by Joyce Lindsay, p. 3)

16 April 1787 - ANDERSON, James and Janie Guerrant, spinster. Sur. Peter Guerrant. (Buckingham County Marriage Bond)

22 December 1814 - ANDERSON, John B. and Nancy G. Bowry. Sur. John G. Bowry. (Charles City County Courthouse records)

6 October 1777 - ANDERSON, Michael and Sally Thomson. (Hanover County Marriage and Ordinary Licenses. Date as reported by Clerk)

24 September 1844 - ANDERSON, Robert, widower, and Miss Mary F. Jordan. (Hanover County Miscellany)

13 October 1846 - ANDERSON, Thomas B., Dr. and Miss Elenora McGhee. (St. Martin's Parish Register, p. 32)

21 December 1831 - ANDERTON, William and Eliza Stacy. (Dinwiddie County, D.B. 1, p. 244, Minister's Return of John Grammer, Jr.)

20 December 1838 - ANDREWS, Abraham and Roberta Crowder. (Dinwiddie County, D.B. 2, p. 302, Minister's Return of James Morrison)

20 August 1845 - ANDREWS, Erasmus and Rebecca B. Scott. (Dinwiddie County, D.B. 5, p. 59, Minister's Return of Hosea Crowder)

25 November 1830 - ANDREWS, John D. and Mrs. Eugenia Thilman. (St. Martin's Parish Register, p. 29)

18 August [1836] - ANDREWS, Mark and Virginia W. Thompson. (Dinwiddie County, D.B. 1, p. 483, Minister's Returns of George A. Bain)

25 March 1835 - ANDUS, Manasseh and Pamelia F. Smith. (Dinwiddie County, D.B. 1, p. 373, Minister's Return of I. E. Hargrave)

16 November 1812 - APPERSON, Richard and _____ [Bride's name not shown] Sur. Wm. M. Murrell. (Charles City County Marriage License)

3

29 July 1823 - ARMSTRONG, William B. and Polly Fox, both of King William County where license was obtained. (Rev. Talley's Register, p. 1)

18 July 1814 - ARMISTEAD, Atkins and Nancy Plumery, daughter of Nancy Plumery who consents. Sur. James Morris. People of Color. (Charles City County Marriage License)

22 December 1798 - ATKINSON, James of New Kent County, and Elizabeth Smith. Thomas Starke, guardian of Elizabeth and consents for her. Sur. Charles Smith. (Marriages of Henrico County, Virginia 1680-1808 by Joyce Lindsay, p. 4)

25 December 1823 - ATKINSON, John S. and Salley Ellett, both of Hanover. (Rev. Talley's Register, p. 2)

16 December 1794 - ATKINSON, Robert of Dinwiddie County and Polly T. Mayo, daughter of William Mayo, Jr. who consents. Sur. Roger Atkinson. (Marriages of Henrico County, Virginia 1680-1808 by Joyce Lindsay, p. 4)

28 December 1831 - ATKINSON, William of Hanover and Elizabeth E. Allen of Henrico. License obtained in Henrico (Rev. Talley's Register, p. 16)

26 October 1848 - AUDRES, Alexander and Susannah C. Lunsford. (Dinwiddie County, D.B. 6, p. 74, Minister's Return of F. A. Gossee)

3 September 1829 - AUSTIN, Obadiah and Miss Jane Clark, both of Hanover County. (Rev. Talley's Register, p. 12)

1 March 1781 - AUSTIN, Thomas and Elizabeth Anderson. (Hanover County Licenses, Marriage and Ordinary. Date as reported by Clerk)

29 January 1825 - AUSTIN, Thomas and Sarah C. Fawcett, both of Hanover County. (Rev. Talley's Register, p. 5)

20 October 1777 - 20 October 1778 - AVERY, John and Joyce Billups. (Gloucester County Licenses, Marriage and Ordinary. Date as reported by Clerk)

B

1 May 1786 - BACON, Nathaniel of New Kent County, and Elizabeth Meux. Sur. William Waddill. (Marriages of Henrico County, Virginia 1680-1808 by Joyce Lindsay, p. 4)

28 February 1786 - BAGWELL, Drury and Catharine Ware of King and Queen County. (Christ Church Parish Register, p. 265)

18 December 1780 - BAILEY, John and Milley Johnson. (Hanover County Licenses, Marriage and Ordinary - date as reported by Clerk)

18 December 1845 - BAILEY, Jno. W. and Nancy P. Major. (Dinwiddie County, D.B. 5, p. 59. Minister's Return of I. E. Hargrave)

22 December 1832 - BAILEY, William of Henrico and Eliza Adams of Hanover. (Rev. Talley's Register, p. 18)

27 July 1787 - BAINE, Warner and Nancy Keiningham of Gloucester. (Christ Church Parish Register, p. 193)

21 November 1849 - BAKER, David, Jr. and Ella Frances Duger, ward of William A. Ellett of King William County. (Virginia Marriage Bonds, Richmond City, by Anne Waller Reddy and Andrew Lewis Riffe IV)

1 August 1851 - BAKER, George F. and Margaret Ann Hays. (Charles City County. These parties married in Camden, New Jersey as per certificate from a Justice of the Peace.)

12 January 1694/5 - BAKER, Moses and Eliz.[a] Browne. Sur. William Crooke. (Elizabeth City D. & W. 1684,1688 and 1702, p. 168)

16 November 1825 - BAKER, Thomas and Alcey Gaulding, both of Hanover. (Rev. Talley's Register, p. 6)

22 December 1836 - BAKER, Thomas, widower, and Miss Rebecca Martin, both of Hanover. (Rev. Talley's Register, p. 24)

20 April 1841 - BALDWIN, James J. and Caroline Bailey. (Dinwiddie County, Marriage Book 1849-67, p. 108)

1 February 1848 - BANISTER, John Munro and Mary Louise Brodnax. (Dinwiddie County, D.B. 5, p.529, Minister's Return of Edmund Withers)

27 December 1833 - BARKER, Charles and Lucy Ann Tucker, both of Hanover. (Rev. Talley's Register, p. 19)

2 July 1834 - BARKER, Edmund and Mary Thacker, both of Hanover. (Rev. Talley's Register, p. 20)

19 January 1825 - BARKER, George and Mildred Lipscomb. License obtained in Hanover. (Rev. Talley's Register, p. 5)

6 November 1845 - BARKER, George, widower, and Miss Mary Wade. (Hanover County Miscellany)

25 January 1841 - BARKER, Jesse of Hanover and Anne Martin. (Virginia Marriage Bonds, Richmond City by Anne Waller Reddy and Andrew Lewis Riffe IV)

5 May 1825 - BARKER, John and Mildred T. Jones, both of Hanover. (Rev. Talley's Register, p. 5)

21 August 1785 - BARLOW, Thomas and Elizabeth James. (Minister's Return of William Leigh, "license in the Borough of Petersburg." Chesterfield County Marriage Register, p. 370)

25 February 1817 - BARLOW, William T. and Susanna Crew, above the the age of twenty-one and who consents. Sur. Elisha Folkes. (Charles City County Marriage License)

5 September 1833 - BARNER, William F. and Elizabeth A. R. Lunsford. (Dinwiddie County, D.B. 1, p. 4, Minister's Return of John Doyle)

3 September 1844 - BARNES, William T. and Elizabeth P. Dabney. (Dinwiddie County, D.B. 5, p. 59, Minister's Return of I. E. Hargrave)

16 March 1846 - BARRICK, James B., bachelor, and Miss Martha Mileston. (Hanover County Miscellany)

11 June 1850 - BARRICKS, Henry and Harriet Wells by I. E. Hargrave. (Dinwiddie County Marriage Book 1849-1867, p. 100)

10 December 1850 - BARROUGH, William L. and Jonathan E[lizabeth] Smith, by I. E. Hargrave. (Dinwiddie County Marriage Book 1849-1867, p. 103)

"1 December 1775 & 1 January 1778" - BATES, Daniel and Elizabeth Bell. (Buckingham County Marriage and Ordinary Licenses - date as reported by Clerk)

14 May 1833 - BATKINS, Bowling, bachelor, and Miss Emily Whitlock, both of Hanover. (Hanover County Miscellany and Rev. Talley's Register, p. 20)

11 November 1842 - BATKINS, Thomas, bachelor, and Mrs. Mary E. Cluvieres. (Hanover County Miscellany)

29 May 1834 - BATKINS, William and Sarah T. West, both of Hanover. (Rev. Talley's Register, p. 20)

18 March 1830 - BATKINS, William and Martha Ann Mantlo, both of Hanover. (Rev. Talley's Register, p. 13)

10 November 1848 - BATTE, Green H. and Adelia R. Bott. (Dinwiddie County D.B. 6, p. 75, Minister's Return of F. A. Gossee)

__ May 1704 - BATTE, William of Prince George, and Mary Stratton. (Marriages of Henrico County, Virginia 1680-1808 by Joyce Lindsay, p. 6)

30 October 1806 - BATTS, Thomas and Betsey Vaughan, daughter of Henry Vaughan who consents. Wit. James Vaughan. (Charles City County License - consent only)

26 March 1792 - BEALE, William C. and Anne Corbin, King and Queen. (Christ Church Parish Register, p. 280)

8th ber 1698 [October] - BEAN, Martin and Ann Allin (?). Return to October General Court 1698. (Elizabeth City County D. & W. 1684,1688, and 1702, p. 168)

17 August 1847 - BEDLOCK, William R. and Griggery C. Challender. (Dinwiddie County, D.B. 5, p. 500 and D.B. 6, p. 118, Minister's Return of Hosea Crowder)

2 September 1846 - BELCHER, James J. and Martha B. Blick, (Dinwiddie County, D.B. 5, p. 188, Minister's Return of Jas. D. Conlling.)

13 April 1802 - BELL, John of Nottoway County and Christiana Roberts. John Freeman, guardian of John Bell. (Amelia County Marriages, p. B-6)

5 da 1 mo [1766] - BELL, Moore, son of George Bell and Rebecka Bell of Hanover County, and Agnes Ellyson of New Kent County, daughter of Joseph Ellyson, dec'd and Mary Ellyson, married at Black Creek Meeting House in New Kent. (White Oak Swamp Friends Records, p. 113)

13 da 10 mo 1684 - BELSON, Edmond, the son of Elizabeth Belson of Nansemond and Mary Crew, the daughter of Mary Tooke of Isle of Wight County, married in the house of his mother. (The Chuckatuck Friends Records, p. 63)

11 da 5 mo 1689 - BELSON, Edmond of Nansemond and Jean Ridick, daughter of Robert Ridick of same county. (The Chuckatuck Friends Records, p. 133)

22 December 1836 - BENNETT, Archibald and Dorothy V. Gibbs. (Dinwiddie County, C.B. 2, p. 115, Minister's Return of John Grammer)

24 December 1833 - BERKELEY, Carter and Ann B. Berkeley. (St. Martin's Parish Register, p. 30)

14 May 1829 - BERKELEY, Edmond and Susan E. Berkeley. (St. Martin's Parish Register, p. 29)

31 August 1837 - BERKELEY, Parke F., Rev. and Miss Mary E. Thweatt of Chesterfield. (St. Martin's Parish Register, p. 30)

5 June 1849 - BERKELEY, Richard F., Dr. and Miss Betty S. Price. (St. Martin's Parish Register, p. 32)

15 December 1831 - BERKELEY, Robert C. and Catherine Smith of Louisa County. (St. Martin's Parish Register, p. 29)

20 December 1838 - BERKELEY, William and Mary Jane Cooke. (St. Martin's Parish Register, p. 30)

28 March 1679 - BEVERLEY, Robert, Major, and Mrs. Katherine Hone, married in Gloucester. (Christ Church Parish Register, p. 18)

8 February 1849 - BEVIL, Thomas and Julian Perkinson, by J. W. Roper. (Dinwiddie County Marriage Book 1849-1867, p. 101)

19 March 1834 - BEVILL, Archer J. and Susan Allen. (Dinwiddie County, D.B. 1, p. 195, Minister's Return of I. E. Hargrave)

14 October 1840 - BEVILL, Claudius P. and Pamelia A. Hardaway. (Dinwiddie County, D.B. 4, p. 126, Minister's Return of T. T. Castleman)

26 April 1855 - BIGGS, John, age 24,widower, born in Accomack County, son of Christopher and Dinney Biggs, and Eliza J. Haynes, 20, single, born in Charles City County, daughter of William and Elizabeth Haynes; married at Bryant's by Henry M. Ammons, M. E. Protestant Church. (Charles City County Courthouse records)

20 October 1777 - 20 October 1778 - BILLUPS, Richard and Lucy Lilley. (Gloucester County Marriage and Ordinary Licenses, date as reported by clerk)

7 da 1 mo 1758 - BINFORD, Aquila, son of Peter and Rebekah Binford of [Prince] George Co. and Mary Ladd, daughter of James and Judith Ladd of Char[les] City County. (White Oak Swamp Friends Records, Acc. #21208, p. 16)

5 da 1 mo. 1777 - BINFORD, James, son of Thomas Binford of
     Prince George County and Hannah Crew, daughter of Andrew
     Crew of Charles City County, married in Waynoak Meeting
     House, Charles City County. (White Oak Swamp Friends
     Records, p. 252)

6 da 12 mo 1772 - BINFORD, Thomas, son of Peter Binford of
     Prince George and Ruth Crew, daughter of Ellyson Crew of
     Charles City, married in Charles City County (White Oak
     Swamp Friends Records, p. 195)

29 November 1799 - BINNS, James of Charles City County, and
     Mrs. Ann Thompson who consents. Sur: John Wells. Wit:
     Michael S. Bradley. (Marriages of Henrico County, Virginia,
     1680-1808 by Joyce Lindsay, p. 8)

20 August 1827 - BINNS, James and Joice Binns, widow of Edmund.
     Sur. Francis Mountcastle. (Charles City County Courthouse
     records)

20 July 1851 - BINNS, James E. and Elizabeth F. Adams. (Charles
     City County Marriage License)

31 March 1852 - BINNS, Richard B. and Elizabeth S. Adams.
     (Charles City County Marriage License)

18 December 1851 - BINNS, Robert F. and Mary Elizabeth Vaiden.
     (Charles City County Marriage License)

23 December 1825 - BINNS, William and Elizabeth Binns. Sur.
     John Binns; Wit. Ro. W. Christian. (Charles City County
     Marriages Box 9, VSL)

18 July 1760 - BIRD, Braxton of King & Queen County and Mary
     Price. Sur. and Wit. John Price and George Bird. (Mid-
     dlesex County Marriage Register, p. 12)

24 August 1812 - BIRD, John and Elizabeth Simpkins. Wit. Wm.
     McGeorge and Wm. Terry. Marriage Agreement. (King William
     County, Book 6, p. 177)

27 May 1847 - BIRDSONG, Nathaniel and Eliza J. Peebles. (Din-
     widdie County, D.B. 5, p. 578, Minister's Return of I. E.
     Hargrave)

24 September 1851 - BISHOP, Chalman C. and Virginia J. Thweatt,
     by R. B. Foster. (Dinwiddie County Marriage Book 1849-
     1867, p. 106)

12 October 1825 - BLACKFORD, William M. and Mary B. Minor,
     Caroline County. (St. Martin's Parish Register, p. 29)

29 October 1851 - BLACKWELL, William F. and Mary A. Ferguson,
     by M. M. Dance. (Dinwiddie County Marriage Book 1849-1867,
     p. 107)

20 October 1777 - 20 October 1778 - BLAKE, Benjamin and Frances
     Currey. (Gloucester County Marriage & Ordinary Licenses,
     date as reported by Clerk)

1 January 1805 - BLAKE, Benjamin of Gloucester County and Mrs.
     Betty Stiff, widow. Sur. and wit. Vincent Yarrington and
     Elizabeth B. Yarrington. (Middlesex County Marriage

8

Register, p. 59)

20 December 1832 - BLAKE, James and Lucy Anderson, both of Hanover. (Rev. Talley's Register, p. 18)

15 April 1787 - BLAND, Ralph and Frances Corr, King and Queen County. (Christ Church Parish Register, p. 265)

14 March 1789 - BLAND, Richard and Mary Bond [or Bowden?], King and Queen County. (Christ Church Parish Register, p. 267)

19 February 1791 - BLAND, Thomas, Jr., and Sarah Waller, King and Queen County. (Christ Church Parish Register, p.268)

20 February 1792 - BLAND, William, Jr., and Mary Ann Corr, King and Queen County. (Christ Church Parish Register, p.197)

19 March 1818 - BLANKS, Thomas and Julia Warburton. Sur. Benjamin Warburton. (Charles City County Marriage License)

20 December 1866 - BLUNT, Mr. _____ and Miss _____ Mallory. (St. Martin's Parish Register, p. 33)

1783 - 1792 - BLYTHE, Jacob and Mary Ann Whitlock. (Hanover County Marriage and Ordinary License, date as reported by clerk)

26 August 1830 - BOAZE, Samuel and Cynthia Jones, both of Hanover. (Rev. Talley's Register, p. 13)

30 December 1685/6 BODGAM or [BLODGAM?], John of Gloucester County and Mary Wallas of this Parish. (Christ Church Parish Register, p. 24)

29 September 1831 - BOGGS, Lewis A. and Eliza Hart, Spotsylvania County. (St. Martin's Parish Register, p. 29)

15 da 12 mo 1727/28 - BOGUE, Wm. of North Carolina and Sarah Duke, daughter of Thomas Duke, late of Nansemond County, dec'd. (Chuckatuck Records [Friends], p. 158)

19 May 1852 - BOISSEAU, Andrew J. and Susan Goodwyn, by I. E. Hargrave. (Dinwiddie County Marriage Book 1849-1867, p. 107)

24 November 1852 - BOISSEAU, James and Sarah J. Wilson, by A. Stewart. (Dinwiddie County Marriage Book 1849-1867, p. 108)

3 May 1842 - BOISSEAU, James P. and Elizabeth A. Scott. (Dinwiddie County, D. B. 3, p. 565, Minister's Return of J. W. Roper)

27 November 1833 - BOISSEAU, John E. and Emily C. Perkins. (Dinwiddie County, D.B. 1, p. 195, Minister's Return of I. E. Hargrave)

__ September 1837 - BOISSEAU, Joseph and Julietta F. Pegram. (Dinwiddie County, D.B. 2, p. 255, Minister's Return of J. W. Roper)

15 November 1842 - BOISSEAU, Joseph G. and Ann G. Clark. (Dinwiddie County, D.B. 3, p. 565, Minister's Return of J. W. Roper)

28 October 1840 - BOISSEAU, Peter and Marianne Mure [Muir].
Dinwiddie County, D.B. 3, p. 609, Minister's Return of
Russel B. Foster)

21 October 1835 - BOISSEAU, Robert and Martha E. Hardaway.
(Dinwiddie County, D.B. 1, p. 373, Minister's Return of
I. E. Hargrave)

15 March 1837 - BOISSEAU, William E. and Julier Grigg. (Dinwiddie County, D. B. 2, p. 255, Minister's Return of
J. W. Roper)

25 September 1783 - BOLES, Peter and Avey Haidy [or Hardy],
King and Queen County. (Christ Church Parish Register,
p. 270)

16 December 1793 - BOLLING, Lenias of Buckingham County, and
Mary Markham, not of age, daughter of Bernard Markham who
consents. Sur. Robert Cary. (Chesterfield County Marriage
Register, p. 37)

8 April 1758 - BOLLING, Robert of Dinwiddie County and Mary
Marshall Tabb. Sur: John Hall. (Amelia County Marriages,
p. B-1)

4 October 1790 - BOLLING, Robert of Petersburg, Dinwiddie
County, and Katharine Stith. Sur. Griffin Stith and
Buckner Stith, Sr. (Brunswick County Marriage Register,
p. 61)

7 April 1783 - BONNER, Richard of Prince George County and
Frances Mitchell, daughter of Mrs. Prissila Northington.
Sur. and Wit. Joshua Young and Joel Rives. (Sussex County
Marriage Register, p. 32)

8 November 1848 - BONNER, Robert (F.N.) and Tabby Bonner (F.N.),
by F. A. Gossee. (Dinwiddie County D.B. 6, p. 75)

22 August 1782 - BOOTH, William and Mary Jones, Gloucester
County. (Christ Church Parish Register, p. 269)

10 January 1844 - BOSHER, James, bachelor, and Miss Jane Nance.
(Hanover County Miscellany)

14 January 1846 - BOSHER, William, Jr., bachelor, and Miss
Judith Talley. (Hanover County Miscellany)

12 February 1833 - BOTT, James H. and Harriet B. H. Hardaway.
(Dinwiddie County, D.B. 1, p. 51, Minister's Return of
W. Hyde)

27 December 1792 - BOWDEN, Robert and Mary Garret, King and
Queen, (Christ Church Parish Register, p. 280)

9 February 1803 - BOWDEN, William of Dinwiddie County, and Eliza
Simmons, 21 years of age. Sur. John Goode, Married 10
February by Rev. Charles Hopkins, Rector, King William
Parish, Episcopal Church, Goochland County. (Powhatan
County Marriage Register, p. 8)

21 September 1803 - BOWLES, Thomas of Hanover County, and
Rebecca Williamson. Sur. John Williamson. (Marriages of
Henrico County, Virginia, 1680-1808 by Joyce Lindsay, p. 10)

28 March 1850 - BOWLS, Henry and Sarah L. Hitchcock, by Hosea
    Crowder. (Dinwiddie County Marriage Book 1849-1867, p. 102)

20 October 1785 - BOWLS, Stubberfield and Sally Collier, King and
    Queen County. (Christ Church Parish Register, p. 264)

26 November 1850 - BOWRY, Henry H. and Bettie Waddill, married
    28 November 1850 by M. J. Sa[illegible]. (Charles City
    County Marriage License)

29 April 1820 - BOWRY, John certifies that he married Major
    Cowl [Coles]. (Charles City Courthouse records)

19 January 1769 - BOWRY, Stephen and Mary Gregory, widow.
    (Charles City Marriage License)

9 September 1826 - BOZE, Thomas H. and Parmelia Warren, both of
    Hanover (Rev. Talley's Register, p. 8)

4 September 1771 - BRADLEY, Benjamin and Martha Hayles, spin-
    ster. Sur. Richard Hayles. (Charles City Marriages,
    Box 9, VSL)

15 November 1805 - BRADLEY, Michael and Elizabeth Otey. Wit.
    James Chandler. Consent only. (Charles City Marriage
    License)

12 February 1811 - BRADLEY, Thomas and Kiddey C. Pond. Sur.
    John Pond; Wit. Edmund Christian. (Charles City Marriages,
    Box 9, VSL)

21 November 1805 - BRADLEY, William and Lucy Pearman. Sur.
    James Nance. (Charles City Courthouse records)

3 December 1856 - BRANCH, James and Martha S. Patteson, Rich-
    mond. (St. Martin's Parish Register, p. 33)

4 November 1835 - BRANDER, John A. and Matilda C. Pegram. (Din-
    widdie County, D.B. 2, p. 115, Minister's Return of John
    Grammer)

22 December 1841 - BRIDGMAN, John J. and Elizabeth A. F. Elder.
    (Dinwiddie County, D.B. 4, p. 407, Minister's Return of
    I. E. Hargrave)

1 May 1833 - BRISTOW, Richard and Ann N. Harmon. (Dinwiddie
    County, D.B. 1, p. 244, Minister's Return of John Grammer,
    Jr.)

26 December 1782 - BROADASS, Reubin and Elizabeth Garland of
    Gloucester County. (Christ Church Parish Register, p. 262)

__ December 1785 - BROADNAX, William and Sarah Jones of Bath
__ Parish by Rev. Thomas Lundie. (Brunswick County Marriage
    Register, p. 347)

23 December 1782 - BROOKE, Christopher of King & Queen County,
    and Elizabeth Saunders. Sur. and wit. Isaac Digges, George
    Saunders and Frances Digges. (Middlesex County Marriage
    Register, p. 26)

7 February 1799 - BROOKE, Humphrey and Sarah Page. William F.
    Gaines, trustee for Sarah Page as to her interest in the

estate of her father, Robert Page, "late of Hanover County."
(King William County, Book 5, p. 316, Marriage Agreement,
recorded 25 April 1809)

9 May 1849 - BROOKS, Joseph N. and Elizabeth Y. Moody. (Dinwiddie County D.B. 6, p. 191, Minister's Return of I. E.
Hargrave)

8 November 1843 - BROWN, Archer J. and Frances J. Tucker (Dinwiddie County, D.B. 4, p. 407, Minister's Return of I. E.
Hargrave)

24 November 1846 - BROWN, Archer J. and Sarah A. Wilson. (Dinwiddie County, D.B. 5, p. 295, Minister's Return of I. E.
Hargrave)

8 September 1801 - BROWN, Basil of King William County, and
Elizabeth P. Price. Sur. John Williamson. (Marriages of
Henrico County, Virginia 1680-1808 by Joyce Lindsay, p. 12)

31 May 1848 - BROWN, Edward G. and Mary F. Thrift. (Dinwiddie
County, D.B. 5, p. 578, Minister's Return of I. E. Hargrave)

22 November 1843 - BROWN, Geo. J. and Mary S. Goodwyn. (Dinwiddie County, D.B. 4, p. 407, Minister's Return of I. E.
Hargrave)

25 April 1764 - BROWN, James of James City County, and Catherine
Cheney. Sur. and Wit. Joseph Tuggle, Elizabeth Elliot, and
John Elliot. (Middlesex County Marriage Register, p. 15)

11 March 1816 - BROWN, James, Jr., son of Dixon, and Sally
Stewart. Sur. Wm. Stewart. People of Color. (Charles
City County Marriage License)

13 June 1833 - BROWN, John T. and Rhoda Thacker, both of Hanover. (Rev. Talley's Register, p. 18)

23 September 1862 - BROWN, Joseph B. and Fanny L. Taylor. (St.
Martin's Parish Register, p. 33)

6 November 1783 - BROWN, Miles and Rachel Jordan, King and
Queen County. (Christ Church Parish Register, p. 263)

6 January 1829 - BROWN, Milton and Elizabeth Walton. (St.
Martin's Parish Register, p. 29)

18 December 1838 - BROWN, Peter E. and Ann C. Waugh. (Dinwiddie County, D.B. 2, p. 529, Minister's Return of I. E.
Hargrave)

27 October 1787 - BROWN, Robert and Lucy Walden. (King & Queen
County, Christ Church Parish Register, p. 193)

28 May 1767 - BROWN, William and Martha Bassett, spinster
(Charles City County, William and Mary Quarterly, v. 8,
p. 195)

20 January 1846 - BROWN, William H. and E. F. Tucker. (Dinwiddie County, D.B. 5, p. 59, Minister's Return of I. E.
Hargrave)

24 December 1779 - BRUSHWOOD, George and Sarah Garrett. (King

and Queen County, Christ Church Parish Register, p. 260)

17 da 2 mo 1688 - BUFKIN, Leaven and Dorrithy Newby, daughter of William Newby of Nanzemund [sic] County, married in his own house. (The Chuckatuck Friends Records, p. 70)

17 March 1790 - BULLINGTON, Wm. and Frances Bradley who consents. Consent only - signed by Frances Bradley. Wit: Elizabeth Jones and John Roper. (Charles City Courthouse records)

12 June 1786 - BONDURANT, Dabney and Lucy Hall, spinster of full age. Thomas Hall, Jr. Surety. (Buckingham County Marriage Bond)

22 June 1763 - BURGE, Drury of Dinwiddie County, son of John Burge, and Elizabeth Dunn, daughter of William Dunn who is Surety. Wit: Joseph Kirkland and John Wynne. (Sussex County Marriage Register, p. 49)

23 December 1805 - BURKE, William and Elizabeth Andrews. Wit: Daniel Powers Keza: Lipscomb and John Whitworth. (King William County, record referring to Marriage Contract dated 28 April 1807, Book 5, p. 89, Reel 4, V.S.L.)

28 February 1828 - BURNETT, Carver and Lucy McDuggle, both of Hanover County. (Rev. Talley's Register, p. 10)

27 April 1837 - BURNETT, Carver, widower, and Miss Elizabeth Wright. (Hanover County, Rev. Talley's Register, p. 25)

26 December 1829 - BURNETT, Coleman and Sarah P. Burnett, both of Hanover. (Rev. Talley's Register, p. 12)

8 January 1833 - BURNETT, Elisha A. and Miss Ann Wade, both of Hanover (Rev. Talley's Register, p. 18)

29 December 1834 - BURNETT, Isaac, bachelor and Miss Sarah Hughes, both of Hanover. Married by Rev. Talley __ January 1835. (Hanover County Marriage and Ordinary Licenses, date as reported by Clerk; also, Rev. Talley's Register, p. 22)

20 October 1831 - BURNETT, Richard and Betsey Hill, both of Hanover. (Rev. Talley's Register, p. 16)

4 October 1832 - BURNETT, William and Eliza Boaze. (Rev. Talley's Register, p. 17)

4 December 1830 - BURNETT, William H. of Hanover and Margaret Hill "of the County". License obtained in New Kent County. (Rev. Talley's Register, p. 14)

26 January 1785 - BURTON, Jacob and Anne Hambleton, daughter of Samuel Hambleton who consents. Sur: Benjamin Goss (Buckingham County Marriage Bond)

3 December 1778 - BURTON, James and Sarah Currey. (King and Queen County, Christ Church Parish Register, p. 195)

23 October 1783 - BURTON, James and Frances Yarrington (King and Queen County, Christ Church Parish Register, p. 263)

31 March 1788 - BURTON, William and Mary Baily. Sur. John Baily.

(Charles City County Marriage Licenses)

13 February 1845 - BURTON, William and Manervie Ann Eckles.
(Dinwiddie County, D.B. 4, p. 768)

21 January 1745 - BURWELL, Lewis, Esq. of James City County and
Mrs. Frances Bray, widow. Sur. and Wit: Henry Thacker.
(Middlesex County Marriage Register, p. 3)

29 May 1789 - BURWELL, Lewis of Gloucester County and Judith
Cannon. John McKeand, guardian of Judith, consents for
her, and is Surety. Wit: Elizabeth McKeand. (Marriages
of Henrico County, 1680-1808 by Joyce Lindsay, p. 14)

28 November 1772 - BURWELL, Nathaniel of James City County and
Susanna Grymes. Sur. and Wit: Philip Grimes and Will
Churchill. (Middlesex County Marriage Register, p. 17)

4 March 1839 - BUTLER, Asa S. to Susanna Seymore. (Dinwiddie
County, D.B. 2, p. 529, Minister's Return of I. E. Hargrave)

27 November 1823 - BUTLER, David S. and Frances J. Dugar, both
of King William County, and license obtained in King William. (Rev. Talley's Register, p. 2)

25 June 1818 - BUTLER, Dick and Mason Booker, by Chas. Roper.
(Dinwiddie County Marriage Book 1849-1867, p. 104)

11 November 1830 - BUTLER, Henry G. and Miss Temperance Coat
of Hanover County. (Rev. Talley's Register, p. 14)

5 da 10 mo 1777 - BUTLER, John, son of William Butler of Dinwiddie County, and Elizabeth Ladd, daughter of James Ladd,
late of Charles City County, dec'd. (White Oak Swamp
Friends Records, p. 263)

13 May 1834 - BUTLER, John T. and Martha A. Tapley. (Dinwiddie
County, D.B. 1, p. 298, Minister's Return of R. B. Foster)

19 September 1849 - BUTLER, John T. and Miss Mildred O. Mallory.
(St. Martin's Parish Register, p. 32)

21 February 1821 - BUTLER, Nelson and Lievelly B. Weymack.
Sur: Edward Carter. (Charles City County Marriages, Box 9,
V.S.L.)

23 August 1826 - BUTLER, Thomas and Nancy Grantland, both of
Hanover. (Rev. Talley's Register, p. 8)

7 November 1832 - BUTLER, Thomas and Mahala Wright, both of
Hanover. (Rev. Talley's Register, p. 18)

1 February 1831 - BUTLER, William and Rebecca Wooddy, both of
Hanover. (Rev. Talley's Register, p. 14)

10 May 1843 - BUTLER, William S. and Frances Hitchcock. (Dinwiddie County, D.B. 4, p. 407, Minister's Return of I. E.
Hargrave)

3 November 1835 - BUTTERWORTH, John W. and Martha E. Abernathy.
(Dinwiddie County, D.B. 1, p. 355, Minister's Return of
Smith Parham)

13 March 1852 - BUZZA (?), Stewart and Rubinella A. Blayton. (Charles City County Marriages)

12 November 1840 - BYRD, George and Sally Ampey. (Dinwiddie County, D.B. 3, p. 96, Minister's Return of I. E. Hargrave)

8 December 1795 - BYRNE, James Jr., of Petersburg, and Sarah S. Haskins, ward of John Haskins. Sur. and wit. Alexander Brown and Jane Simmons. (Brunswick County Marriage Register, p. 88)

C

17 July 1840 - CABELL, Henry J. and Miss Arabella B. Vaughan. (St. Martin's Parish Register, p. 30)

7 December 1848 - CAIN, James K. and Elizabeth M. Jackson. (Dinwiddie County, D.B. 6, p. 46, Minister's Return of W. O. Bailey)

24 October 1837 - CALLIS, John W. of Mathews County, and Miss Virginia Ann Gibson, married 24 October 1837 by L. W. Allen Minister's return only. (Middlesex County Marriage Register, p. 164)

20 October 1777 to 20 October 1778 - CAMP, Thomas and Rebeccah Dobson. (Gloucester County Licenses, Marriage and Ordinary date as reported by clerk)

18 December 1826 - CAMPBELL, William and Elizabeth A. Minor. (St. Martin's Parish Register, p. 29)

26 January 1826 - CANE, John M. and Caroline Hill, Caroline County. (St. Martin's Parish Register, p. 29)

25 November 1791 - CARDER, John and Cathajane Davis. Sur: Benjamin Davis. (Buckingham Marriage Bonds)

28 January 1779 - CARDWELL, James and Ann Eubank, King and Queen County. (Christ Church Parish Register, p. 195)

8 May 1833 - CARDWELL, James W. and Emily Neal. (Dinwiddie County, D.B. 1, p. 298, Minister's Return of R. B. Foster)

8 January 1694/5 - CAREY, Thomas of Warwick County, and Eliz^{a} Hinds. (Elizabeth City County, D. & W. 1684, 1688, and 1702, p. 168)

19 March 1789 - CARLTON, Beverley and Caty Drummond, King and Queen. (Christ Church Parish Register, p. 266)

— February 1778 - CARLTON, Humphrey and [bride's name not shown]. (King and Queen County Licenses, Marriage and Ordinary, date as reported by clerk)

25 August 1843 - CARPENTER, William and Sarah J. Fulcher. (St. Martin's Parish Register, p. 30)

20 June 1809 - CARTER, Ishmael and Elvey Martin, who conents, Sur: Freeman Brown and Wit: John Gregory and Isaac Ratcliff. (Charles City County Marriage Licenses)

21 May 1779 - CARTER, Jeduthan of King and Queen County, and

15

Sally Carter. Sur: Jesse Carter. (Powhatan County Marriage Register, p. 2)

15 May 1779 - CARTER, Jesse and Hannah Baylor, King and Queen (Christ Church Parish Register, p. 260.

12 January 1787 - CARTER, John and Elizabeth Collins. Sur. and wit. Benjamin Morris and Peter Royster. (Charles City County Marriages)

30 November 1842 - CARTER, William B., bachelor and Miss Caroline E. Thomas. (Hanover County Licenses, Marriage and Ordinary)

31 January 1785 - CARY, Miles and Grizzet Buxton of Nansemond County, daughter of Thomas Buxton. Robert Cowper, guardian of Grizzett. Sur: James Gray. (Southampton County Marriage Register, p. 40)

4 December 1783 - CASTLEN, Andrew of Hanover County and Ann Turner of same County, widow of George Turner. Wit: Jedidiah Turner and James Blackwell. (Hanover Court Records 1783-1792, p. 14. Note: The date is the recorded date of the agreement, not necessarily the marriage date)

9 November 1696 - CEELEY, Cha: and Eliza. Saunders. Return to General Court 1697. (Elizabeth City Deeds and Wills 1684, 1688, 1702, p. 168)

8 April 1840 - CHADICK, Richard, widower, and Miss Catharine McGhee. (Hanover County Miscellany)

4 October 1828 - CHADICK, Thomas D. and Sarah Martin. License obtained in New Kent County and parties live in said County. (Rev. Talley's Register, p. 11)

5 January 1788 - CHANCY, William and Mary Timberlake, who consents. (Charles City Courthouse records. This is consent only)

30 October 1837 - CHANDLER, Asa and Mary Phillips by John Lattimore. (Dinwiddie County, D.B. 2, p. 6)

22 December 1841 - CHANDLER, Benjamin and Mary A. Traylor. (Dinwiddie County, D.B. 3, p. 565, Minister's Return of J. W. Roper)

16 June 1825 - CHANDLER, George and Rebecca E. Armistead. Sur: Wm. B. Christian. (Charles City County Marriage Licenses)

27 November 1843 - CHANDLER, William D. and Elizabeth L. Sandifer. (Dinwiddie County, D.B. 5, p. 390, Minister's Return of J. W. Roper)

29 August 1854 - CHAPIN, _____ and Miss Virginia Evans, Richmond. (St. Martin's Parish Register, p. 32)

11 June 1789 - CHAPMAN, Henry and Ann Bland, King and Queen County. (Christ Church Parish Register, p. 267)

7 January 1788 - CHAPMAN, Joseph of Gloucester County, and Jane Foard, widow of William Ford. Sur. John Robins. (Marriages of Richmond County, Virginia 1668-1853 by

16

George H. S. King, p. 35)

29 July 1845 - CHAPPELL, George W. and Mrs. Maria Wade. (Hanover County Miscellany)

21 November 1759 - CHAPPELL, Robert of Dinwiddie County, and Agnes Cross, with consent of William Cross. Sur: Daniel Jones. (Amelia County Marriage Register, C-1)

27 January 1831 - CHAPPILL, William and Jane Boze, both of New Kent County. (Rev. Talley's Register, p. 14)

10 da 7 mo 1768 - CHARLES, Thomas, son of Henry Charles, dec'd of Charles City County, and Lydia Ladd, daughter of James Ladd, married in Charles City County. (White Oak Swamp Friends Records, p. 157)

12 April 1786 - CHASTAIN, Stephen and Mary Amonet, daughter of William Amonet who consents. Sur: John Eldridge. (Buckingham County Marriage Bonds)

23 December 1841 - CHESTERMAN, Edwin H. and Mary C. Jenkins, daughter of Catharine Jenkins of Hanover County. (Virginia Marriage Bonds, Richmond City, by Anne Waller Reddy and Andrew Lewis Riffe IV, p.76)

21 May 1835 - CHILDERS, Nathaniel, widower, and Mrs. Gilley Vines, both of Hanover County. (Rev. Talley's Register p. 22 and Hanover County Miscellany)

21 April 1835 - CHILDRESS, Francis, widower, and Miss Eveline R. Meredith. (Hanover County Miscellany)

7 December 1777 - CHILES, Thomas and Mary James. (Hanover County Licenses, Marriage and Ordinary, date as reported by clerk)

3 June 1772 - CHRISTIAN, Charles and Rebecca Terrill. William Christian consents. (Charles City County, William and Mary Quarterly, v. 8, p. 194)

13 October 1778 - CHRISTIAN, Charles and Mary Mitchell, widow Sur: Henry Vaughan. (Charles City County Courthouse records)

3 February 1768 - CHRISTIAN, John and Mary Maynard. (Charles City County, William and Mary Quarterly, v. 8, p. 195)

10 da 4 mo 1759 - CHUNING [CHEWNING], Joseph of Caroline County and Jemima Johnson, daughter of David Johnson of Hanover County. (White Oak Swamp Friends Records, p. 28)

5 April 1827 - CLAIBORNE, George Dr., of King William, and Mary M. Craig. (Virginia Marriage Bonds, Richmond City, by Anne Waller Reddy and Andrew Lewis Riffe IV, p. 38)

16 November 1834 - CLARDY, Meredith C. and Elizabeth Talley, by R. B. Foster. (Dinwiddie County D.B. 1, p. 298)

11 February 1845 - CLARDY, Pleasant and Martha Ann Vaughan. (Dinwiddie County, D.B. 4, p. 768, Minister's Return of F. B. Foster)

6 January 1836 - CLARKE, Asa and Nancy Perkinson. (Dinwiddie County, D.B. 1, p. 417, Minister's Return of W. Hyde)

6 November 1855 - CLARKE, Colin D. and Bettie B. Cooke. (St. Martin's Parish Register, p. 32)

7 October 1842 - CLARKE, George and Elizabeth Lawson, who consents. Sur: Littleberry Vaughan. (Charles City County Marriage Register)

24 December 1850 - CLARKE, John B. and Mary J. Jones. (Dinwiddie County, Marriage Book 1849-67, p. 104)

22 December 1851 - CLARKE, John D. and Elizabeth _____. (Charles City County Marriage Register)

9 November 1846 - CLARKE, Nathan B., bachelor and Miss Martha B. Allen. (Hanover County Miscellany)

8 June 1838 - CLARKE, Samuel H. and Mary C. Kidd. (Dinwiddie County, D.B. 2, p. 517, Minister's Return of Russel B. Foster)

4 March 1851 - CLARK, Thomas J. and Arithma R. Puckett by Hosea Crowder. (Dinwiddie County Marriage Book 1849-67, p. 107)

25 May 1791 - CLARK, William and Frances Taylor, spinster of Full age. Sur: Thomas McCormack. (Buckingham County Marriage Bond)

4 September 1781 - CLARKE, William and Anny Lennard, daughter of William Lennard. Consent only. (Charles City County Marriage Register)

4 December 1845 - CLARKE, William W. and Ann E. Foard. (Dinwiddie County, D.B. 5, p. 59, Minister's Return of I. E. Hargrave)

17 July 1838 - CLAY, Edward and Sarah Lester. (Dinwiddie County, D.B. 2, p. 517, Minister's Return of Russel B. Foster)

13 November 1783 - CLAYTON, James and Jane Dillard, King and Queen County. (Christ Church Parish Register, p. 263)

8 December 1842 - CLAYTON, John and Mary A.F.M. Thweatt. (Dinwiddie County, D.B. 4, p. 407, Minister's Return of I. E. Hargrave)

14 February 1826 - CLEGG, Hillary of King and Queen County, and Sarah Waide of Hanover County. (Rev. Talley's Register, p. 7)

12 February 1851 - CLEMENTS, Benjamin H. and Rebecca C. Hawks. (Dinwiddie County Marriage Book 1849-67, p. 106)

29 December 1783 - CLOPTON, David of New Kent County, and Mary Ann Vandervall who consents. Sur: Nicholas Giles. (Marriages of Henrico County, Va. 1680-1808 by Joyce Lindsay, p. 19)

16 January 1838 - CLOPTON, Henley D., bachelor, of New Kent County and Miss Mary Parsons of Hanover. (Hanover County

Miscellany and Rev. Talley's Register, p. 26)

5 January 1781 - CLOPTON, Robert and Fanny Anderson. (Hanover County Licenses, Marriage and Ordinary. Date as reported by Clerk)

8 March 1832 - CLOPTON, William of New Kent County and Celina H. R. Acree of Henrico County. License obtained in Henrico County. (Rev. Talley's Register, p. 17)

16 November 1782 - COATS, Robert and Mary Spann of Gloucester County. (Christ Church Parish Register, p. 262)

___ da 12 mo. 1808 - COBBS, Thomas, son of Pleasant Cobbs of Caroline County and Martha Stanley, daughter of Littleberry Stanley of Hanover County. (Cedar Creek Friends Records, Marriage Certificates 1799-1808)

19 February 1851 - COFER, Jesse H. and Edmona C. Stagg. Married 20 February 1851 by Rev. B. F. Woodward of the M.E. Church South. (Charles City Marriage Register)

5 January 1694/5 - COFIELD, William of Nansimun [sic] and Eliza Sheppard. (Elizabeth City County, D. and W. 1684, 1688, and 1702. p. 168)

12 January 1782 - COLEMAN, John and Dorothy Wyatt of Gloucester County. (Christ Church Parish Register, p. 261)

11 March 1851 - COLGIN, George W. and Elizabeth J. Binns. (Charles City Marriage Register)

26 March 1791 - COLLIER, Benjamin and Rachel Ware, King and Queen County. (Christ Church Parish Register, p. 268)

10 May 1792 - COLLIER, Francis and Susannah Dillard, King and Queen County. (Christ Church Parish Register, p. 257)

14 April 1782 - COLLY, Charles and Elizabeth Hudson, King and Queen County. (Christ Church Parish Register, p. 269)

9 December 1835 - COOK, James Henry and Locky James Daniel. (Dinwiddie County, D.B. 1, p. 373, Minister's Return of I. E.Hargrave)

5 June 1784 - COOK, Thomas and Kitty Meredith, King and Queen County. (Christ Church Parish Register, p. 263)

11 January 1798 - COOK, Thomas of Gloucester and Rachel Murray Beverley Yates. Married 15 January 1799 by Henry Heffernan. [Consent dated 10 January 1799.] Thomas Roane, guardian of Rachel. Sur. and Wit.: George Murray. (Middlesex County Marriage Register, p. 47)

3 May 1832 - COOKE, William and Martha B. Smith, Louisa County. (St. Martin's Parish Register, p. 30)

22 December 1847 - CORBETT, James and Miss Louisa C. W. George, Caroline County. (St. Martin's Parish Register, p. 32)

19 November 1839 - CORBIN, Robert B. of Caroline County and Mary C. Mills, daughter of Nicholas Mills, Esq. (Virginia Marriage Bonds, Richmond City, by Anne Waller Reddy and

Andrew Lewis Riffe IV, p. 70)

15 February 1838 - CORLING, Charles and Manerva S. Thompson.
(Dinwiddie County, D.B. 2, p. 517, Minister's Returns of
Russel B. Foster)

27 April 1841 - CORNWELL, James S. and Julia A. Leach. (Dinwiddie County, D.B. 3, p. 96, Minister's Return of I. E.
Hargrave)

24 October 1786 - CORR, John and Frances Campbell (King and
Queen County). (Christ Church Parish Register, p. 265)

15 November 1838 - COSBY, William H. and Amanda F. Marshall.
(St. Martin's Parish Register, p. 30)

29 May 1780 - COTTRELL, William and Nancy Reynolds. Sur. and
Wit.: John Reynolds and Jno. Quarles, Jr. (Copy of Mar-
riage Bond from King William County from the John K. Martin
Papers, V.S.L.)

11 March 1830 - COURTNEY, William H. and Maria M. Anderson, both
of New Kent County. (Rev. Talley's Register, p. 13)

17 November 1851 - COUSINS, William and Mary A. Goodwyn. (Dinwiddie County Marriage Book 1849-67, p. 106)

29 April 1845 - COX, John P. and Louisa M. P. Wells. (Dinwiddie County, D.B. 4, p. 768, Minister's Return of R. B.
Foster)

17 April 1844 - COX, William and Ruth Ann Grigg. (Dinwiddie
County, D.B. 4, p. 768, Minister's Return of R. B. Foster)

15 January 1820 - CRADDOCK, John and Susan H. Taylor, daughter
of G. B.Taylor who consents. Sur: William Griffin.
(Charles City County Marriage Register)

30 April 1851 - CRAIG, James R. Dr. and Miss Lucy Ann Bolling
by W. E. Webb. (Dinwiddie County Marriage Book 1849-67,
p. 104)

6 September 1851 - CRENSHAW, Edwin P. and Olivia E. Stubblefield, married 10 September 1851 by Rev. B. F. Woodward
of the M. E. Church South. (Charles City County Marriage
Register)

6 da 8 mo 1776 - CREW, Andrew, son of Andrew Crew of Charles
City County and Mary Binford, daughter of John Binford of
Charles City County. (White Oak Swamp Friends Records,
p. 246)

4 January 1813 - CREW, Elijah and Sally Evans. Sur: Jonathan
Evans. (Charles City Marriage Register)

7 da 9 mo 1773 - CREW, James, son of John Crew of Charles City
County, and Ann Crew, daughter of Ellyson Crew of Charles
City County. (White Oak Swamp Friends Records, p. 210)

9 da 11 mo 1773 - CREW, John, son of Ellyson Crew, dec'd, of
Charles City County and Judith Crew, daughter of John Crew
of Charles City County. (White Oak Swamp Friends Record,
p. 213)

3 da 12 mo 1775 - CREW, Macajah, son of Joseph Crew of Caroline County, dec'd, and Margaret Ladd, daughter of James Ladd, of Charles City County, dec'd. (White Oak Swamp Friends Record, p. 245)

10 April 1824 - CREW, Robert and Nancy Kerbey, both of Hanover County. (Rev. Talley's Register, p. 3)

29 October 1831 - CREW, Robert, widower, and Sarah Adams, spinster. (Hanover County Miscellany)

12 November 1831 - CREW, Robert and Sarah Martin, both of Hanover County. (Rev. Talley's Register, p. 16)

17 December 1789 - CRITTENDEN, John and Polly Ware, King and Queen. (Christ Church Parish Register, p. 267)

22 December 1781 - CRITTENDON, Richard and Frances Sykes of King and Queen County. (Christ Church Parish Register, p. 261)

20 June 1782 - CRITTENDEN, Zachariah and Elizabeth Ware, King and Queen County. (Christ Church Parish Register, p.269)

13 January 1819 - CROFORD, Norman and ____ Hitchcock. (Dinwiddie County Marriage Book 1849-67, p. 105)

20 February 1834 - CROSS, Richard D. and Elizabeth B.Wells. (Dinwiddie County, D.B. 1, p. 244)

24 August 1836 - CROSS, William O. to Sarah K. Hooper of Hanover, his ward. (Virginia Marriage Bonds, Richmond City, by Anne Wallor Reddy and Andrew Lewis Riffe IV, p. 58)

12 November 1836 - CROWDER, Albert and Mary Page Hunter by W. Hyde. (Dinwiddie County, D.B. 1, p. 417)

25 December 185? - CROWDER, Alphus and Susanna Andrews by Hosea Crowder. This marriage apparently should be 1850 since it is followed by the same minister's next marriage which took place in January 1851. (Dinwiddie County Marriage Book 1849-1867, p. 106)

4 February 1845 - CROWDER, Bolin and Susan Tally by Hosea Crowder. (Dinwiddie County, D.B. 5, p. 59)

29 October 1818 - CROWDER, Chamer and Sarah Caudle by Chas. Roper. (Dinwiddie County Marriage Book 1849-1867, p.104)

23 October 1845 - CROWDER, Collin and Martha Stowe by Hosea Crowder. (Dinwiddie County, D.B. 5, p. 59)

21 November 1844 - CROWDER, Herbert and Mary C. Clay by Jos. W. Roper. (Dinwiddie County, D.B. 5, p. 390)

19 December 1833 - CROWDER, Hosiea and Mary A. Dance by W. Hyde. (Dinwiddie County, D.B. 1, p. 51)

18 December 183? - CROWDER, James M. and Pamelia Crowder by W. Hyde. (Dinwiddie County, D. B. 1, p. 417)

16 December 1847 - CROWDER, John N. and Minerva J. Hudson by Hosea Crowder. (Dinwiddie County, D.B. 6, p. 118;

also D.B. 5, p. 500)

8 December 1842 - CROWDER, Joseph and Harriet F. Lewis by J. W.
Roper. (Dinwiddie County, D.B. 3, p. 565)

13 February 1837 - CROWDER, Nathaniel and Paskey G. Burnett by
Russel B. Foster. (Dinwiddie County D.B. 2, p.517)

14 June 1848 - CROWDER, Nelson and Frances Sturdivant by I. E.
Hargrave. (Dinwiddie County, D.B. 5, p. 578)

27 November 1850 - CROWDER, Nevvel and Harriet Crowder by J. W.
Roper. (Dinwiddie County Marriage Book 1849-67, p. 105)

8 April 1846 - CROWDER, Theodorick and Lucinda F. P. Pool by
I. E. Hargrave. (Dinwiddie County, D.B. 5, p. 295)

18 March 1833 - CROWDER, Thomas T. and Jane Andrews by W. Hyde.
(Dinwiddie County, D.B. 1, p. 51)

11 March 1819 - CROWDER, William J. and Rebecca Roper by Chas.
Roper. (Dinwiddie County Marriage Book 1849-67, p. 105)

30 October 1837 - CROWDER, Willis and Caroline Phillips by John
Lattimore. (Dinwiddie County, D.B. 2, p. 6)

5 May 1847 - CRUMP, Cornelius L. and Mary Bradley Crump by John
G. Carter. (Dinwiddie County, D.B. 5, p. 295)

11 December 1832 - CRUMP, John P. and Susan M. Wynn by John
Grammer, Jr. (Dinwiddie County, D.B. 1, p. 244)

19 September 1784 - CRUMP, Richard of Williamsburg, and May
Gafford. (Marriages of Surry County, Virginia 1768-1825
by Catherine L. Knorr)

5 November 1812 - CRUMP, William, Dr. of Powhatan, and Maria
Moody, orphan of Phillip Moody of Williamsburg. (Virginia
Marriage Bonds, Richmond City, by Anne Waller Reddy and
Andrew Lewis Riffe IV, p.16)

29 October 1779 - CRUTCHFIELD, Lewis and Mildred Jamison, spinster. (Charles City County, William and Mary Quarterly,
v. 8, p.194)

31 March 1825 - CRUTCHFIELD, Peter and Elizabeth W. Hooper,
both of Hanover. (Rev. Talley's Register, p. 5)

7 August 1660 - CUNDIFEE, John and Johan Mountain, Parish of
Martin Brandon. (Charles City County, Virginia Colonial
Abstracts 11, p. 92 and p. 270 Order Book)

24 August 1776 - CURLE, William B. [or R.] Wilson and Sarah
Lyon. (Elizabeth City County Licenses, Marriage and
Ordinary. Date as reported by Clerk)

___ October 1791 - DABNEY, Benjamin and Sarah Smith, King and
Queen County. (Christ Church Parish Register, p. 268)

2 December 1834 - DABNEY, William and Julia A. R. Sydnor by
R. B. Foster. (Dinwiddie County, D.B. 1, p. 298)

6 April 1848 - DANCE, Alexander A. and Elizabeth Williamson by

Hosea Crowder. (Dinwiddie County, D.B. 6, p. 118)

19 November 1835 - DANDRIDGE, Bolling of Goochland County and
   Laura E. Dudley of New Kent County. License obtained in
   New Kent. (Rev. Talley's Register, p. 23)

22 February 1782 - DANDRIDGE, John of Hanover and Elizabeth
   Booth, daughter of Thos. Booth who consents. Sur. and Wit.
   Robert Dandridge. (Marriages of Henrico County, Virginia
   1680-1808 by Joyce H. Lindsay, p. 25)

10 April 1845 - DANIEL, John and Creasy Andrews by I. E. Hargrave. (Dinwiddie County, D.B. 5, p. 59)

26 December 1849 - DANIEL, Reuben and Lovely Crowder by Hosea
   Crowder. (Dinwiddie County Marriage Book 1849-1867, p.102)

18 June 1793 - DANIEL, William and Polly Martin, daughter of
   Martin Martin [sic] who consents. (Charles City Courthouse
   records)

23 March 1831 - DARRACOTT, Richard F. and Mary N. Berkeley.
   (St. Martin's Parish Register, p. 29)

____ 1768 - DARRICOT, William of Hanover and Catherine
   Finch of Petsworth Parish. (Kingston Parish Register,
   p. 226)

28 May 1785 - DAVENPORT, Reubin and Jane Crump, King William
   County. (Christ Church Parish Register, p. 264)

22 January 1824 - DAVENPORT, William and Frances Ann Milestone,
   both of Hanover. (Rev. Talley's Register, p. 3)

15 November 1792 - DAVIDSON, David and M____ Phillips who
   consents. (Charles City County Marriage Licenses, Box 9,
   VSL)

10 December 1835 - DAVIDSON, Thomas of Richmond and Miss Coley
   White of Hanover. (Rev. Talley's Register, p. 23)

1 March 1757 - DAVIS, Andrew, Jr. of Gloucester County,
   bachelor, and Lucia Staige, spinster. Sur. and Wit.
   William Young of Essex County and Robert Allcock. (Middlesex Marriage Register, p. 10)

19 February 1835 - DAVIS, Edward A. and Milly Williams by
   I. E. Hargrave. (Dinwiddie County D.B. 1, p. 373)

14 November 1833 - DAVIS, Hartwell and Ann M. Williams by
   R. B. Foster. (Dinwiddie County, D.B. 1, p. 298)

2 August 1827 - DAVIS, Herman and Ann S. James. (St. Martin's
   Parish Register, p. 29)

7 da 8 mo 1775 - DAVIS, Mi[c]ajah, son of John Davis of Louisa
   County and Mary Johnson, daughter of David Johnson of
   Hanover County. (White Oak Swamp Friends Records, p. 233)

28 February 1792 - DAVIS, Staige and Elizabeth Gardner, King
   and Queen County. (Christ Church Parish Register, p. 197)

26 January 1842 - DAVIS, Stephen and Susan P. Elder by J. W.

Roper.   (Dinwiddie County, D.B. 3, p. 565)

5 April 1698 - DAVIS, Witten (?) and Rebecah Skinner (?).
   (Elizabeth City County D. & W. 1684,1688 and 1702, p.168)

12 June 1847 - DAY, Pleasant and Elizabeth Jane White who
   consents. Sur. Pleasant Jerdon. (Charles City County
   Marriage Licenses)

19 April 1838 - DEJARNETTE, Wm. Y. and Miss Cora Williamson.
   (St. Martin's Parish Register, p. 30)

25 March 1849 - DELANEY, William T. and Martha A.E.T. Spain
   by J. W. Roper. (Dinwiddie County Marriage Register
   1849-1867, p. 101)

13 June 1840 - DENEGRI, John B. and Sarah Jane Burruss, daugh-
   ter of Elizabeth Vaughan of Caroline County. (Virginia
   Marriage Bonds, Richmond City, by Anne Waller Reddy and
   Andrew Lewis Riffe IV, p. 71)

5 March 1764 - DENNIS, Wm. of James City County and _____
   daughter of Wm. Parrish. Wit. Wm. Parrish, Jr. and Samuel
   Parrish. Consent only. (Charles City Marriage Register)

20 da 12 mo 1723 - DENSON, Wm., son of John Denson of Isle of
   Wight County and Amey Small, daughter of Benj: Small of
   Nansemond County. (Chuckatuck Friends Records, p.152)

3 July 1687 - DEPREE, Abraham and Rebecca Smith both of old
   Rappahannock County. (Christ Church Parish Register, p. 35)

19 May 1851 - DeWITT, Thos. H. and Miss Betty A. Fontaine. (St.
   Martin's Parish Register, p. 32)

22 December 1787 - DIDLAKE, James and Mary Gardner, King and
   Queen County. (Christ Church Parish Register, p. 266)

26 December 1789 - DIDLAKE, Philip and Lucy Falkner, King and
   Queen County. (Christ Church Parish Register, p. 267)

7 January 1787 - DIDLAKE, William and Lucy Boyd, King and Queen
   County. (Christ Church Parish Register, p. 265)

2 May _____ - DIDLICK, Robert and Mary Baker, King and Queen
   County. (Christ Church Parish Register, p. 198)

26 March 1835 - DIGGS, Ralph W. and Miss Lucy C. Smith. (St.
   Martin's Parish Register, p. 30)

30 December 1778 - DILLARD, Thomas and Mary Dillard, King and
   Queen County. (Christ Church Parish Register, p. 195)

30 October 1823 - DIXON, James of New Kent County and Lucy
   Barker of Hanover. License obtained in New Kent County.
   (Rev. Talley's Register, p. 2)

16 January 1783 - DIXON, Michael and Catharine Didlake of King
   and Queen County. (Christ Church Parish Register, p.262)

28 December 1863 - DOSWELL, B. T. and Laura C. Doswell. (St.
   Martin's Parish Register, p. 33)

27 December 1827 - DOSWELL, Benjamin F. and Maria B. Doswell. (St. Martin's Parish Register, p. 29)

20 January 1847 - DOSWELL, George W. and Miss Ann Elizabeth Taylor. (St. Martin's Parish Register, p. 32)

25 October 1827 - DOSWELL, Hendley C. and Evelina O. Harris. (St. Martin's Parish Register, p. 29)

12 January 1864 - DOSWELL, Henly C. and Mrs. Fanny J. B. Terry. (St. Martin's Parish, p. 33)

3 May 1845 - DRAKE, Robert and Mary Jane Tucker. Sur. Richard Tucker. (Charles City County Marriage License, Box 9, V.S.L.)

8 November 1832 - DRAPER, Charles and Louisa M. Withers by John Grammer, Jr. (Dinwiddie County D.B. 1, p. 244)

24 December 1823 - DREWEY, George and Elizabeth N. Powell, both of King William County. (Rev. Talley's Register, p. 2)

24 January 1848 - DREW, William C. and Mary V. Ann Vines, daughter of Lucy Vines of Petersburg. (Virginia Marriage Bonds, Richmond City, by Anne Waller Reddy and Andrew Lewis Riffe IV, p. 96)

22 July 1844 - DRISCOLL, Dennis O. and Mrs. Frances Southworth. (St. Martin's Parish Register, p. 30)

20 October 1777 - 20 October 1778 - DRIVER, John and Dorothy Treacle. (Gloucester County Marriage and Ordinary Licenses-date as reported by clerk)

11 December 1849 - DRIVER, John and Mary T. Wells by I. E. Hargrave. (Dinwiddie County Marriage Book 1849-1867, p. 100)

8 March 1791 - DRUMMOND, Samuel and Isbell Gibson, King and Queen County. (Christ Church Parish Register, p. 268)

18 July 1679 - DUDLEY, James and Mary Welch, married in Gloucester. (Christ Church Parish Register, p. 18)

13 May 1775 - DUDLEY, Thomas of the County of King and Queen and Mrs. Mary Curtis of this parish. (Kingston Parish Register, p. 232)

19 December 1789 - DUDLEY, Thomas and Betsey Shepard Crittenden, King and Queen County. (Christ Church Parish Register, p. 267)

3 January 1833 - DUKE, Alfred and Ann E. Goodwin. (St. Martin's Parish Register, p. 30)

4 July 1839 - DUKE, Albert N. and Mary E. Harding, Louisa. (St. Martin's Parish Register, p. 30)

8 da 3 mo 1701 - DUKE, Tho: of Nansemond "took a wife contrary to the Scriptures... and that was not of us." (The Chuckatuck Friends Records, p. 92)

4 February 1773 - DULANY, Benjamin of Anapolis, Maryland and

Elizabeth French, "under 21, about 17", spinster. Penelope French, widow, and George Mason, Esq., guardian and trustee of Elizabeth. Marriage Agreement. (Fairfax County D.B. Liber K-L (1772-1773), pp. 342-346)

17 February 1787 - DUNCAN, Fleming and Martha Scruggs, of full age. Sur. Pleasant Saunders. (Buckingham County Marriage Bond)

21 June 1809 - DUNCAN, Joseph C., 21 years of age of Buckingham County, and Ann Stratton, daughter of John Stratton; married 22 June by Rev. Samuel Woodfin. William Stratton guardian of Ann and Surety. (Powhatan County Marriage Register, p. 63)

___ May 1776 - DUNLOP, Wm. and _____ [bride's name not shown]. King and Queen Licenses, Marriage and Ordinary, date as reported by clerk)

15 January 1806 - DUNN, James and Catharine McTyre, above 21 years. Ann Dunn of Essex County, guardian of James. Sur. and Wit. Thomas Ussery and William Parron. (Middlesex Marriage Register, p. 61)

20 October 1777 - 20 October 1778 - DUN, John and Mary Forrest. (Gloucester County Licenses, Marriage and Ordinary, date as reported by clerk)

8 April 1694/5 - DUNN, Pascho and Hannah Powers. (Elizabeth City County, D. & W. 1684,1688 and 1702, p. 168)

10 October 1796 - DUNN, William of Prince George County and Jane Ligon. Married 20 October by Rev. Needler Robinson, Rector of Dale Parish Episcopal Church. Sur. William Baugh. (Chesterfield County Marriage Register, p. 45)

30 May 1781 - DUNSTON, Warner and Susanna Brooking, Gloucester County. (Christ Church Parish Register, p. 261)

E

13 March 1838 - EANES, Ammonett and Ann Hunnicutt by I. E. Hargrave. (Dinwiddie County D.B. 2, p. 529)

1 August 1839 - EARNEST, George L., Jr., widower of King William County and Miss Agness Huges [Hughes] of Hanover County. (Rev. Talley's Register, p. 26)

11 March 1831 - EARNIST, John H. and Lucy Ann Whitlock, both of Hanover. (Rev. Talley's Register, p. 15)

31 April 1699 - EDLOE, John of James City County, and Martha Hatcher. (Marriages of Henrico County, Virginia 1680-1808 by Joyce Lindsay, p. 28)

6 March 1833 - EDMUNDS, Nicholas and Mary Ann Moody, by I. E. Hargrave. (Dinwiddie County D.B. 1, p. 4)

22 December 1800 - EDWARDS, Ambrose and Barbary Finch. Sur. Thos. Edwards, Aaron Q. Starke. Wit. Ambrose Edwards Nicholas Johnson, Waller Burke, and Lain J. Moring. (Fragment of a marriage contract. King William County, Book 4, p. 25)

21 November 1767 - EDWARDS, Edward of Prince George County and
Bea Brockwell. Sur. Augustine Claiborne, (Sussex County
Marriage Register, p. 11)

23 May 1850 - EDWARDS, John H. and Mary Ann Thrift by I. E.
Hargrave. (Dinwiddie County Marriage Book 1849-1867,
p. 100)

15 October 1785 - EDWARDS, William and Nancy Robinson, Gloucester. (Christ Church Parish Register, p. 264)

8 June 1839 - EDWARDS, Wm. N. H. and Susan E. Jackson by Joseph
W. D. Creath. (Dinwiddie County D.B. 2, p. 528)

4 January 1838 - ELDER, Austin C. and Eliza Ann Kirtland by
Isham E. Hargrave. (Dinwiddie County D.B. 2, p. 37)

2 June 1843 - ELDER, George and Martha A. Davis by R. B. Foster.
(Dinwiddie County D.B. 4, p. 768)

27 December 1838 - ELIOT, Nathaniel and Elizabeth Brantern by
J. W. Roper. (Dinwiddie County D.B. 2, p. 255)

29 May 1787 - ELLETT, Robert of Hanover County and Lucy Morgan
of New Kent County. Sur. Pleasant Bradley. (Charles City
County Marriage Licenses, Box 9, V.S.L.)

13 March 1828 - ELLETT, Temple and Mary W. Acree, both of New
Kent County. Licenses obtained in New Kent County. (Rev.
Talley's Register, p. 10)

29 March 1828 - ELLIOTT, John and Melvina Adeline Archer, both
of Hanover. (Rev. Talley's Register, p. 10)

29 May 1787 - ELLIOTT, Robert of Hanover and Lucy Morgan of
New Kent. (Hanover County Licenses - Marriages and
Ordinary, date as reported by clerk. See ELLETT, Robert)

20 December 1827 - ELLYSON, Daniel of New Kent County and Martha
A. Wade of Hanover. (Rev. Talley's Register, p. 10)

4 June 1829 - ELLYSON, Havilah and Elizabeth Acree, both of
New Kent County. (Rev. Talley's Register, p. 12)

6 da 11 mo 1766 - ELLYSON, Isaiah, son of William and Jane
Ellyson of New Kent County, and Cisilia Wooddy, daughter
of Micajah and Cisilia Wooddy of Hanover County. Married
in a publick meeting appointed for that purpose at the
Meeting House of the above said County of Hanover. (White
Oak Swamp Friends Records, p. 125)

17 January 1848 - ELLYSON, James F. and Jane E. A. Roffe, by
I. E. Hargrave. (Dinwiddie County D.B. 6, p. 191)

7 da 5 mo 1772 - ELLYSON, John, son of Robert Ellyson of New
Kent County, and Agnes Woodson, daughter of Charles Woodson
of Henrico County. (White Oak Swamp Friends Records,
p. 192)

16 da 12 mo 1778 - ELLYSON, Thomas of New Kent County, and
Agnes Ellyson, daughter of Gideon Ellyson of New Kent
County. (White Oak Swamp Friends Records, p. 282)

10 da 6 mo 1762 - ELLYSON, William, son of William Ellyson, and Molly Johnson, daughter of Nathan Johnson of New Kent County. (White Oak Swamp Friends Records, p.63)

30 May 1811 - ENNIS, John of Petersburg, and Mary D. Hare, daughter of John D. Hare who consents. Sur. William G. Wills. (Chesterfield County Marriage Register, p. 109)

5 June 1845 - ENOS, William H. of Gloucester County, and Mary Elizabeth Walker, daughter of Joel Walker. Married by George Northam. Sur. and Wit. John T. West and Francis M. Walker. (Middlesex County Marriage Register, p. 128)

8 May 1828 - EPPES, John T. of Hanover and Sarah Ann Fox of King William. (Rev. Talley's Register, p. 10)

23 May 1825 - EPPES, Peter T. and Catharine Heath, both of Hanover. (Rev. Talley's Register, p. 6)

7 June 1804 - EUBANK, Philip of King William and Elizabeth P. Tignor. Sur. Thomas Bosher. Wit. Thomas New, Thomas Hughes, and Benjamin Gary. (Marriage contract, King William County Book 4, p. 249)

29 April 1830 - EVANS, Batty H. and Ann H. Young by John Grammer, Jr. (Dinwiddie County D. B. 1, p. 244)

27 August 1844 - EVANS, Batty H. and Susanna M. Ledbetter by W. J. Norfleet. (Dinwiddie County D.B. 4, p. 768)

F

30 September 1834 - FALKNER, Benjamin M., bachelor and Miss Catherine H. Tyree, both of Hanover. Married 2 October 1834 by Rev. Charles Talley. (Hanover County Miscellany and Rev. Talley's Register, p. 21)

7 September 1788 - FARGUESON, Thomas and Ann Didlake, King and Queen County. (Christ Church Parish Register, p. 266)

17 August 1812 - FARLEY, Stephen and Elizabeth P. Allen, daughter of Richard Allen of Nottoway County who consents. Sur. Edmund Morris. (Amelia County Marriage Register, p. F-3)

25 September 1848 - FAUNTLEROY, Samuel G., Jr. of King and Queen County, and Fanny B. Claybrook, daughter of M. E. Claybrook. Married 5 October 1848 by R. A. Christian. Sur. and Wit. William L. Claybrook and Z. L. Claybrook. (Middlesex County Marriage Register, p. 135)

4 January 1781 - FEAR, Henry and Sarah Lipscombe. (Hanover County Licenses, Marriage and Ordinary. Date as reported by clerk)

__ November 1687 - FEARNE, John of Gloucester and Mary Lee of this parish. (Christ Church Parish Register, p.38)

19 September 1783 - FEILD, Theophilus of Prince George County and Martha Simmons, widow. Sur. Richard Elliott. (Brunswick County Marriage Register, p. 31)

7 May 1840 - FEILD, Theophilus A. and Lucy O. Thweatt by T. T. Castleman. (Dinwiddie County D.B. 4, p. 126)

3 August 1836 - FENN, Allen and Martha F. E. Scott by Isham E. Hargrave. (Dinwiddie County D.B. 2, p. 37)

30 March 1797 - F[igg]?, John and Susanna Collier, Gloucester County. (Christ Church Parish Register, p. 336)

15 December 1845 - FISHER, James W.D.W. and Harriet A.E. Mitchel, by J. W. Roper. (Dinwiddie County D.B. 5, p.391)

14 February 1843 - FISHER, Pleasant H. and Mary P. Reames, by R. B. Foster. (Dinwiddie County D.B. 4, p. 768)

__ January 1778 - FLEMING, Carter and ____ [bride's name not shown]. (King and Queen County Licenses, Marriage and Ordinary. Date as reported by clerk)

21 November 1833 - FLETCHER, Matthew M. and Martha H. Scott, by John Grammer, Jr. (Dinwiddie County D.B. 1, p. 244)

14 September 1781 - FLIPPEN, John and Elizabeth Carney, Kingston Parish, Gloucester County. (Christ Church Parish Register, p. 261)

3 February 1834 - FLOCKHART, John of Petersburg and Jane Banks. (Virginia Marriage Bonds, Richmond City, by Anne Waller Reddy and Andrew Lewis Riffe IV, p. 52)

13 December 1838 - FOARD, Joseph M. and Ann E. Spain by James Morrison. (Dinwiddie County D.B. 2, p. 302)

28 January 1787 - FORBES, Alexander and Lucy Scruggs, of lawful age. Sur. Bartlett Davis. (Buckingham County Marriage Bond)

5 November 1850 - FORD, Jeremier and Ariadne E. Tucker, by J. W. Roper. (Dinwiddie County Marriage Book 1849-1867, p. 105)

5 September 1801 - FORD, John of Hanover County and Judith Butler. (Virginia Marriage Bonds, Richmond City, by Anne Waller Reddy and Andrew Lewis Riffe IV, p. 2)

26 May 1802 - FORD, Lankston of Hanover County and Elizabeth Jones. Sur. John Burton. (Marriages of Henrico County, Virginia 1680-1808 by Joyce Lindsay, p. 32)

20 October 1777-20 October 1778 - FORREST, Josiah and Sarah Foster. (Gloucester County Licenses - marriage and ordinary. Date as repoted by clerk)

21 February 1843 - FOSTER, James B. and Sarah M. Burton, orphan of Jack T. Burton, dec'd and ward of Miles Tunstall of New Kent. (Virginia Marriage Bonds, Richmond City, by Anne Waller Reddy and Andrew Lewis Riffe IV, p. 79)

20 October 1777-20 October 1778 - FOSTER, Jesse and Catherine Foster. (Gloucester County Licenses - marriage and ordinary. Date as reported by clerk)

20 October 1777-20 October 1778 - FOSTER, John and Elizabeth Culley. (Gloucester County Licenses - marriage and ordinary. Date as reported by clerk)

6 April 1824 - FOSTER, John H. of Richmond, and Sarah A.E.C.
   Clopton of New Kent County. (Rev. Talley's Register, p. 3)

10 June 1775 - FOSTER, Richard of Hanover County, and Judith
   Walker. Sur. Edmund Walker. (Amelia County Marriage Register p. F-1)

12 February 1824 - FOSTER, William of King William County, and
   Susan White of Hanover. (Rev. Talley's Register, p. 3)

5 May 1831 - FOSTER, William, widower, of Hanover, and Frances
   T. Burton of New Kent. (Rev. Talley's Register, p. 15)

24 November 1836 - FOSTER, Xavier S. and Lucy Ann Ledbetter, by
   John Grammer. (Dinwiddie County D.B. 2, p. 115)

5 November 1834 - FOUNTAINE, James and Juliet C. Morris of
   Louisa. (St. Martin's Parish Register, p. 30)

27 August 1808 - FOX, Nathaniel of King William County, and
   Susan Bockins, widow, who signs her own consent. (Mar-
   riages of Henrico County, Virginia 1680-1808, by Joyce
   Lindsay, p. 32)

16 February 1789 - FRASER, Alexander and Dicey Shackleford.
   Marriage contract. (Dinwiddie County Order Book 1789-1791,
   p. 4)

18 _____ 1834 - FRASER, Frederick R. and Edna B. Rogers.
   (Dinwiddie County D.B. 1, p. 298)

17 December 1840 - FRASER, Robert B. and Martha C. Wainwright
   by Russel B. Foster. (Dinwiddie County D.B. 3, p. 609)

1 March 1806 - FRAYSER, Benjamin and Nancy Parrish, a Free
   Mulatto woman. Benjamin was emancipated by George Frayser
   of Hanover County. Sur. Isham Winn. (Marriages of Henrico
   County, Virginia 1680-1808, by Joyce Lindsay, p. 33)

12 February 1778 - FRAZIER, William and Elizabeth Mitchell.
   (Hanover County Licenses, Marriage and Ordinary. Date as
   reported by clerk)

2 June 1824 - FREEMAN, Robert and Ann Hunnicutt, who consents.
   Sur. Elisha Crew; Wit. R. F. Graves. (Charles City
   Marriage License)

7 May 1833 - FRENCH, Thomas, bachelor, and Miss Lucretia Wade,
   both of Hanover County. Married 9 May 1833 by Rev. Talley.
   (Hanover County Miscellany and Rev. Talley's Register,
   p. 18)

G

6 December 1777 - GARDNER, John and Anna Richardson. (Hanover
   County Licenses, Marriage and Ordinary; date as reported
   by clerk)

16 April 1787 - GARLAND, John of Hanover County, and Nancy
   Crawley, sister of David Crawley who is her guardian and
   gives his consent. Sur. Isaac Holmes. (Amelia County
   Marriage Register, G-1)

18 December 1783 - GARRET, Edmond and Nancy Didlake, King and Queen County. (Christ Church Parish Register, p. 263)

4 November 1773 - _____, _____ and Franky Garrett, King and Queen County. Groom's name not shown. (Christ Church Parish Register, p. 201)

15 March 1848 - GARRETT, James W. and Miss Mary S. Anderson, by George W. Langhorne. (Dinwiddie County D.B. 6, p. 41)

11 December 1784 - GARROTT, Charles and Cloe Agee, spinster, of full age. Sur. John Agee. (Buckingham County Marriage Bond)

30 April 1806 - GATHRIGHT, Theoderick and Elizabeth Jordan. Sur. Anderson Jordan; wit. E. Christian. (Charles City County Marriage License)

27 December 1845 - GARTHRIGHT, Benjamin and Margaret Ann Gaulding. (Hanover County Miscellany)

4 July 1833 - GARY, Thomas of Richmond and Miss Nancy Milestone of Hanover. (Rev. Talley's Register, p. 20)

9 December 1843 - GAULDIN, William E. and Miss Emeline Tucker. (Hanover County Miscellany)

20 October 1777 - 20 October 1778 - GAYLE, Thomas and Mary Culley. (Gloucester County Licenses, Marriage and Ordinary; date as reported by clerk)

7 February 1778 - GENTRY, Benjamin Carter Waller and Miss Catherine Page. (Hanover County License, Marriage and Ordinary)

23 March 1826 - GENTRY, Henry of King and Queen County, and Joanna Kerby of Hanover. (Rev. Talley's Register, p.8)

10 da 6 mo 1799 - GEORG, Edward and Sarah Smyth, married at house of Robert Pleasants. (Friends Records Marriage Certificates 1799-1808, Cedar Creek Meeting, Hanover)

16 June 1696 - GEORGE, John of Nansemond County and Francis Servant. (Elizabeth City County D. & W. 1684,1688, and 1702, p. 168)

20 December 1843 - GIBBS, Freeman and Dorothy Miles, by I. E. Hargrave. (Dinwiddie County D.B. 4, p. 407)

22 November 1838 - GIBS, Peter and Sarah Young by J. W. Roper. (Dinwiddie County D.B. 2, p. 255)

1 December 1841 - GIBBS, Robert and Jane W. Miles, by I. E. Hargrave. (Dinwiddie County D.B. 4, p. 407)

20 July 1830 - GIBSON, John and Nancy Via, both of Hanover. (Rev. Talley's Register, p. 13)

26 December 1839 - GIBSON, John, widower, and Miss Emily G. Mileston. (Hanover County Miscellany)

21 January 1843 - GIBSON, William, bachelor, and Miss Henrietta J. Jones. (Hanover County Miscellany)

26 March 1818 - GILL, William and Mary Crew. Sur. Henry B. Christian. (Charles City County Courthouse records)

18 October 1847 - GILLIAM, Thomas B. and Julia A. Foster, by John D. Southall. Marriage recorded on this date, not necessarily marriage or license date. (Dinwiddie County D.B. 5, p. 390)

31 December 1845 - GITTMAN, Andrew and Ann Crow, by J. W. Roper. (Dinwiddie County D.B. 5, p. 391)

27 November 1849 - GITTMAN, William W. and Harriet J. Polan, by J. W. Roper. (Dinwiddie County Marriage Book 1849-1867, p. 102)

25 December 1823 - GLASS, Thomas and Sarah Butler, both of Hanover. (Rev. Talley's Register, p. 2)

11 November 1790 - GLOVER, John Jr. of Nansemond County and Polly Darden, daughter of Robert Darden. Sur. and Wit. John Wood and S. Kello. (Southampton County Marriage Register, p. 68)

30 November 1843 - GOGGIN, James and Susan Medlin, by I. E. Hargrave. (Dinwiddie County D.B. 4, p. 407)

6 March 1791 - GOINGE, Henry and Betsey Paggot, King and Queen County. (Christ Church Parish Register, p. 268)

__ September 1763 - GOODRICH, Benjamin and Mary Tyree, spinster, daughter of Mary Tyree who is also guardian and who consents. Wit. William Dancy and Francis Tyree. (Charles City County Courthouse records)

27 January 1853 - GOODWIN, William H. and Miss Julia Ann Goodwin. (St. Martin's Parish Register, p. 32)

23 December 1847 - GOODWYN, Algernon S. and Adelina V. Lewis, by I. E. Hargrave. (Dinwiddie County D.B. 5, p. 578)

8 November 1849 - GOODWYN, John P., Dr. and Martha E. Greenway, by J. W. Arnold. (Dinwiddie County Marriage Book 1849-1867, p. 100)

1 May 1833 - GOODWYN, William H. and Harriet L. Williamson, by I. E. Hargrave. (Dinwiddie County D.B. 1, p. 4)

1 December 1775 - 1 January 1778 - GOOLSBY, William and Frances May. (Buckingham County Licenses, Marriage and Ordinary. Date as reported by clerk)

21 December 1826 - GORDON, William H. and Eliza M. Willcox. Eliza E. Willcox gives consent. Sur. Richard T. Long. Wit. J. E. Timberlake and H. McClure. (Charles City County courthouse records)

27 October 1696 - GORINGE, Charles and Elynor Allanby. (Elizabeth City County D. & W. 1684, 1688, and 1702, p. 168)

30 October 1785 - GOSS, William and Dicey Kidd, spinster, of full age. Sur. Isaac Salle. (Buckingham County Marriage Bond)

31 May 1688 - GOUGH, William of New Kent County and Alice Thacker of this Parish. (Christ Church Parish Register, p. 41)

5 December 1849 - GRAMMER, John H. and Martha J. Wells, by
I. E. Hargrave. (Dinwiddie County Marriage Book 1849-1867,
p. 100)

25 October 1780 - April 1781 - GRANTLAND, Gideon and Sarah
Bradford. (Hanover County Licenses, Marriage and Ordinary.
Date as reported by clerk)

3 July 1828 - GRANTLAND, John of Richmond and Miss _____ Acree
of New Kent County. License obtained in Henrico County.
(Rev. Talley's Register, p. 10)

25 December 1811 - GRAVES, Benjamin of Nottoway County and
Milly F. Hancock. William Hancock, brother of Milly, con-
sents for her and is surety. (Marriages of Chesterfield
County, Virginia by Catharine Knorr, p. 61)

20 July 1848 - GRAVES, Benj. C. and Elizabeth C. Graves, daughter of Ro. W. Graves. Sur. Richard M. Graves and Wit.
Edm'd Christian. (Charles City Marriage Licenses)

21 August 1783 - GRAVES, Richard of Dinwiddie County and Dolly
Blunt, daughter of Richard Blunt, dec'd. William Blunt,
guardian. Sur. William Mason. (Sussex County Marriage
Register, p. 33)

11 November 1835 - GREEN, Henry G. and Sarah T. Browder, by
I. E. Hargrave. (Dinwiddie County D.B. 1, p. 373)

13 November 1832 - GREEN, Shadrack and Sally N. Heath, by
Augustine Heath. (Dinwiddie County D.B. 1, p. 26)

27 January 1830 - GREEN, William T. and Mary Cathirine Oliver,
both of Hanover. (Rev. Talley's Register, p. 12)

22 December 1841 - GREEN, William H. and Susan[ah?] Nutall.
(St. Martin's Parish Register, p. 30)

3 August 1774 - GREGORY, John and Elizabeth Maynard. (Charles
City County, William & Mary Quarterly, v. 8, p. 194)

4 April 1807 - GREGORY, John and Mary Shields. Sur. Sylvanus
Gregory. (Charles City County Courthouse records)

24 July 1764 - GREGORY, William and Anne Royster, spinster.
Sur. Thomas Holt. (Charles City Marriage License)

18 Sept. 1786 - GRIFFIN, Jachariah and Elizabeth Beverley, both
free mulattos. Sur. William Fuqua. (Buckingham County
Marriage Bond)

__ April 1778 - GRIFFITH, Joseph and _____ [bride's name not
shown]. (King and Queen County Licenses, Marriage and
Ordinary. Date as reported by clerk)

11 April 1836 - GRIGG, George W. and Ann E. Lewis, by Russel B.
Foster. (Dinwiddie County D.B. 2, p. 517)

3 September 1850 - GRIGG, Humphrey C. and Mary A. B. Tucker,
by J. M. Arnold. (Dinwiddie County Marriage Book

1849-1867, p. 100)

19 December 1849 - GRIGG, Joseph W. and Indiana F. Tucker, by J. M. Arnold (Dinwiddie County Marriage Book 1849-1867, p. 100)

16 December 1841 - GRIGG, Williamson B. and Mary A. L. Niblett, by I. E. Hargrave. (Dinwiddie County D.B. 4, p. 407)

6 August 1791 - GROOM, James and Frances Finley, King and Queen County. (Christ Church Parish Register, p. 268)

14 February 1783 - GROOM, John and Elizabeth Curry of King and Queen County. (Christ Church Parish Register, p. 262)

21 April 1791 - GROOM, Richard and Catharine Webb, King and Queen County. (Christ Church Parish Register, p. 268)

1 June 1835 - GRUBBS, Claiborne, bachelor, and Miss Catharine Clarke. Married 21 June 1835 by Rev. Charles Talley. (Hanover County Miscellany and Rev. Talley's Register, p.22)

31 May 1834 - GRUBBS, Henry and Frances Tucker, both of Hanover. (Rev. Talley's Register, p. 20)

11 August 1830 - GRUBBS, William and Miss Sarah Hazelwood, both of Hanover. (Rev. Talley's Register, p. 13)

20 October 1777 - 20 October 1778 - GRYMES, Charles and Mary Hubard. (Gloucester County Licenses, Marriage and Ordinary. Date as reported by clerk)

16 December 1858 - GRYMES, William T. and Cornelia H. Corker. (St. Martin's Parish Register, p. 33)

28 March 1782 - GUTHRIE, James and Nancy Garrett of King and Queen County. (Christ Church Parish Register, p. 261)

H

8 December 1791 - HAINES, John of Nottoway County and Martha Walker of Lunenburg County. Married 8 December 1791 by John Jones of Nottoway. (Lunenburg County W.B. 4, p.20)

8 July 1835 - HALL, Albert P. and Eliza B. Nunnally, by I. E. Hargrave. (Dinwiddie County D.B. 1, p. 373)

20 October 1777 - 20 October 1778 - HALL, Francis and Johannah Hall. (Gloucester County Licenses, Marriage and Ordinary. Date as reported by clerk)

24 June _____ HALL, James and Mary Walden, King and Queen County. (Christ Church Parish Register, p. 198)

7 da 11 mo 1707 - HALL, Moses and Margrett Duke. Thomas Duke father of Margrett and who consents. (The Chuckatuck Friends Records, p. 37)

"Between 20 October 1777 - 20 October 1778" - HALL, William and Catherine Wiatt. (Gloucester County Licenses, Marriage and Ordinary. Date as reported by clerk)

17 July 1848 - HALL, William and Susan Wynn, by F. A. Gossee.

(Dinwiddie County D.B. 6, p. 75)

26 December 1787 - HALYARD, William and Frances Stedman, King
and Queen County. (Christ Church Parish Register, p.266)

27 May 1811 - HAMBLETT, Arthur and Susan Crutchfield, who consents. Consent only. (Charles City Marriage License)

22 August 1844 - HAMILTON, John T. and Marion A. Vaughan, by
I. E.Hargrave. (Dinwiddie County D.B. 5, p. 59)

12 January 1832 - HAMMON, James E. and Martha Evans, by John
Grammer, Jr. (Dinwiddie County D.B. 1, p. 244)

7 August 1780 - HANSIL, William and Judith Crew. (Charles City
County, William & Mary Quarterly, v. 8, p. 195)

29 November 1834 - HARDA (?), Andrew and Frances M. Perkinson
by I. E. Hargrave. (Dinwiddie County D.B. 1, p. 195)

17 August 1849 - HARDAWAY, John and Elizabeth Hogwood, by J. W.
Roper. (Dinwiddie County Marriage Book 1849-1867, p. 102)

24 November 1783 - HARDAWAY, Robert of Dinwiddie County, and
Sarah Hicks, daughter of James Hicks, Sr. Sur. Isaac
Hicks. (Brunswick County Marriage Register, p. 31)

30 March 1836 - HARDAWAY, Robert R. and Jane Thweatt, by J. W.
Roper. (Dinwiddie County D.B. 2, p. 255)

28 November 1833 - HARDAWAY, Stith and Elizabeth Ann Young,
by I. E. Hargrave. (Dinwiddie County D.B. 1, p. 195)

7 March 1752 - HARDEE, John of Gloucester County, and Michal
Sutton, who was born 11 January 1728, and is the daughter
of Christopher and Hope Sutton. Sur. and Wit. William
Segar. (Middlesex County Marriage Register, p. 6)

7 May 1775 - HARDIMAN, William Jr. of Charles City County and
Ann Dent Black, daughter of William Black. Sur. Archibald
Blair and Wit. Anne Blair. (Chesterfield County Marriage
Register, p. 4)

12 April 1784 - HARDYMAN, Littleberry and Elizabeth Eppes.
(Charles City County, William & Mary Quarterly, v. 8, p.194)

20 October 1863 - HARFIELD, William and Sarah C. Perkins. (St.
Martin's Parish Register, p. 33)

26 November 1850 - HARGRAVE, I. E. Rev. and Jane S. Wyatt, by
Wm. B. Rowzie. (Dinwiddie County Marriage Book 1849-1867,
p. 103)

19 June 1839 - HARGRAVE, James, Jr. and Harriet C. Chappell,
by I. E. Hargrave. (Dinwiddie County D.B. 2, p. 529)

10 da 9 mo 1776 - HARGRAVE, Jesse, son of Samuel and Martha
Hargrave of Caroline County, and Mary Pleasants, daughter
of John and Agnes Pleasants of Henrico County. (White Oak
Swamp Friends Records, p. 247)

8 September 1845 - HARMAN, Ithama [sic], widower and Miss Ann
Mantlo. (Hanover County Miscellany)

30 July 1836 - HARPER, Colston T. and Martha J. Tucker, by
Russell B. Foster. (Dinwiddie County D.B. 2, p. 517)

21 December 1778 - HARPER, Joseph of Dinwiddie County, and
Elizabeth Lambert, widow. Sur. Drury Mathis. (Brunswick
County Marriage Register, p. 20)

23 December 1835 - HARRIS, Harrison and Polly Wright, by I. E.
Hargrave. (Dinwiddie County D. B. 1, p. 373)

22 December 1836 - HARRIS, John G. and Miss Mary Y. Williamson.
(St. Martin's Parish Register, p. 30)

8 da 11 mo 1761 - HARRIS, Obediah, son of Benjamin Harris of
Hanover County and Rebecca Johnson, daughter of David
Johnson of same county. (White Oak Swamp Friends Records,
p. 64)

20 Nov. 1815 - HARRIS, Patrick H. and Elizabeth Harris, daughter of John Harris of Buckingham County. Sur. Obadiah
Lockett. Wit. Mary Harris. Married 23 November by Rev.
John Wooldridge. (Powhatan County Marriage Register,
p. 77)

17 December 1849 - HARRIS, Thomas of King and Queen County,
and Betsy Key, daughter of Thomas Key. Sur. and Wit.
Joseph Key, William L. Gatewood, and William K. Gatewood.
(Middlesex County Marriage Register, p. 137)

24 November 1853 - HARRIS, Thomas H. and Miss Betty F. Martin.
(St. Martin's Parish Register, p. 32)

20 December 1780 - HARRIS, William and Diana Goodwin. (Hanover
County Licenses, Marriage and Ordinary. Date as reported
by clerk)

18 April 1826 - HARRISON, Braxton and Cammila A. M. Johnson,
Sur. Thos. E. Poythress. (Charles City County Marriage
License)

6 November 1855 - HARRISON, John P. and Nannie Cooke. (St.
Martin's Parish Register, p. 32)

7 August 1775 - HARRISON, Lemuel of Prince George County, and
Susanna Eppes, daughter of Edward Eppes. Sur. and wit.
Benjamin Baird and Sarah Tomlinson. (Sussex County
Marriage Register, p.21)

16 November _____ - HARRISON, Trent E. and Mary C. Clark, by
Russel B. Foster. (Dinwiddie County D.B. 3, p. 609)

25 December 1782 - HART, James and Milly Gest of King and
Queen County. (Christ Church Parish Register, p. 262)

Xber ye 2 96[sic] - HARVIE, Thomas and the widow Hendrick.
Returned to General Court October 21, 1696. (Elizabeth
City County D. & W. 1684, 1688, and 1702, p. 168)

20 December 1821 - HARWOOD, John T. and Mildred Morecock. Sur.
William New. (Charles City Marriage Licenses)

7 September 1695 - HARWOOD, Tho. Mr. and Mrs. Ann Wythe, Senr.
(Elizabeth City County D. & W. 1684, 1688, and 1702, p. 168)

18 May 1844 - HARWWOD, Thomas, Bachelor, and Miss Lucretia White. (Hanover County Miscellany)

11 December 1839 - HASKINS, Richard Edward and Mary Amanda Thweatt, by I. E. Hargrave. (Dinwiddie County D.B. 2, p.529)

16 February 1847 - HASTINGS, Peter and Elizabeth J. Bishop, by I. E. Hargrave. (Dinwiddie County D.B. 5, p. 295)

13 November 1844 - HASTINGS, Thomas and Ann Adams, by I. E. Hargrave. (Dinwiddie County D.B. 5,p. 59)

7 April 1831 - HAW, Richardson T. and Margaret M. Watt, both of Hanover County. (Rev. Talley's Register, p. 15)

18 December 1849 - HAWKINS, Burzeller H. and Frances E. Vaughan, by I. E. Hargrave. (Dinwiddie County Marriage Book 1849-1867, p. 100)

10 July 1833 - HAWKINS, Gardner and Sarah Roberts, by I. E. Hargrave. (Dinwiddie County D.B. 1, p. 4)

24 December 1840 - HAWKINS, James and Almedia Hoste, by I. E. Hargrave. (Dinwiddie County D.B. 3, p. 96)

29 November 1851 - HAWKINS, James E. and Minerva Maitland, by I. E. Hargrave. (Dinwiddie County Marriage Book 1849-1867, p. 106)

9 February 1846 - HAWKINS, Robt. and Sarah P. Vaughan, by I. E. Hargrave. (Dinwiddie County D.B. 5, p. 59)

25 January 1843 - HAWKINS, Wm. H. and Martha J. Thrift, by I. E. Hargrave. (Dinwiddie County D.B. 4, p. 407)

20 December 1848 - HAWKS, Benjamin and Julia A. P. Pool, by I. E. Hargrave. (Dinwiddie County D.B. 6, p. 191)

26 January 1845 - HAWKS, Thomas and Sarah B. Slaughter, by J. W. Roper. (Dinwiddie County D.B. 5, p. 391)

10 September 1785 - HAXALL, William and Elizabeth Jones. Minister's Return of William Leigh, "license from Dinwiddie County." (Chesterfield County Marriage Register, p. 370)

3 November 1781 - HAYES, Thomas and Mary Buckner Walker, Gloucester County. (Christ Church Parish Register, p. 261)

29 January 1827 - HAYES, William S. and Lucy A. Waddill, daughter of William H. Waddill, who consents. Sur. John W. Bradley. (Charles City County Courthouse records)

16 October 1824 - HAYNES, Edward B., son of Wm. C. Haynes, and Frances A. E. Hall. Sur. Wm. C. Haynes. (Charles City County Marriage Licenses)

2 March _____ - HAYNES, George and Susannah Waller, King and Queen County. (Christ Church Parish Register, p. 198)

14 January 1830 - HAZLEGROVE, William and Ann P. Oliver, both of Hanover County. (Rev. Talley's Register, p. 12)

3 April 1833 - HEATH, Allen I. and Tabitha J. Butterworth, by
Augustine Heath. (Dinwiddie County D.B. 1, p. 26)

21 August 1850 - HEATH, John and Virginia E. Tucker, by J. M.
Arnold. (Dinwiddie County Marriage Book 1849-1867, p. 100)

9 May 1845 - HEATH, Richard, widower, and Miss Sarah Ann Tuck.
(Hanover County Miscellany)

9 March 1791 - HENINGHAM, Benjamin and Rose Berryman Shackelford, King and Queen County. (Christ Church Parish Register, p.207)

8 October 1777 - HENRY, Patrick, Esq. and Miss Dorothea Dandridge. (Hanover County Licenses - Marriage and Ordinary,
date as reported by clerk)

24 December 1827 - HIGGINS, Foster and Rebecca Bailey, both of
New Kent County. License obtained in Henrico County.
(Rev. Talley's Register, p. 10)

6 April 1835 - HILL, Charles and Lucy Wilson, people of color,
by John Grammer, Jr. (Dinwiddie County D.B. 1, p. 244)

26 November 1840 - HILL, Edmund H. and Miss Ann Elizabeth
Smith, Louisa. (St. Martin's Parish Register, p. 30)

9 March 1834 - HILL, Edwin and Eliza Minor, Caroline County.
(St. Martin's Parish Register, p. 30)

22 April 1851 - HILL, Nathan and Mary Miles, free negroes, by
J. B. Spiers. (Dinwiddie County Marriage Book 1849-1867,
p.105)

28 February 1839 - HILL, Richard and Maria Malone, by I. E.
Hargrave. (Dinwiddie County D.B. 2, p. 529)

22 March 1786 - HILL, Robert and Sally Anderson, spinster.
William Anderson, father of Sally consents and is Surety.
(Buckingham County Marriage Bonds)

29 December 1851 - HILL, Robert and Joanna Bonner, free negroes,
by F. A. Gosee. (Dinwiddie County Marriage Book 1849-
1867, p. 106)

27 December 1834 - HILL, Robert W. of New Kent County and Miss
Martha Wright of Hanover County. (Rev. Talley's Register,
p. 21)

19 April 1832 - HILL, Thomas of King William and Elizabeth G.
Walker of New Kent County. (Rev. Talley's Register, p. 17)

15 September 1824 - HILLIARD, Benjamin and Jenny Johnson. Sur.
Ludwell Brewer. (Charles City County Marriage License)

30 March 1791 - HINES, Christopher and Ann Young, who consents.
Sur. Benjamin McWilliams. (Charles City County Marriage
License)

27 December 1836 - HITCHCOCK, Isham and Mary W. Storr, by
W. Hyde, (Dinwiddie County D.B. 1, p. 534)

13 January 1819 - HITCHCOCK, Joel and Mary Nance, by Chas.

Roper.   (Dinwiddie County Marriage Book 1849-1867, p. 105)

10 May 1837 - HITCHCOCK, John G. and Julia M. Adams, by Isham E.
   Hargrave. (Dinwiddie County D.B. 2, p. 37)

20 October 1777 - 20 October 1778 - HOBDAY, Richard and Anne
   White.   (Gloucester County License - Marriage and Ordinary.
   Date as reported by clerk)

14 August 1834 - HOBSON, Matthews of Henrico, and Elizabeth W.
   Crutchfield, widow, of Hanover County. (Rev. Talley's
   Register, p. 21)

10 da 10 mo 1765 - HOGG, Thomas of Hanover County and Martha
   MacGhee, daughter of Samuel MacGhee, dec'd of same county.
   (White Oak Swamp Friends Record, p. 109)

30 January 1834 - HOGWOOD, Alexander and Elizabeth Lewis, by
   I. E. Hargrave. (Dinwiddie County D.B. 1, p. 195)

4 July 1850 - HOGWOOD, David R. and Martha P. Wynn, by J. W.
   Roper. (Dinwiddie County Marriage Book 1849-1867, p.105)

29 January 1781 - HOLLINGS, George and Nancy Lewis. (Hanover
   County Licenses - Marriage and Ordinary. Date as reported
   by clerk)

7 da 8 mo 1680 - HOLLOWELL, Henry, son of Tho: Hollowell of
   Elizabeth River County [sic, probably Elizabeth City] and
   Elizabeth Cotching, daughter of Thos. Cotching of Chucka-
   tuck, Nansemond County, deceased. Among witnesses: Tho:
   Hollowell, father; Alice Hollowell, mother; two brothers,
   Tho. Hollowell, Junr., Phil Howard; two mothers, Alice
   Hollowell, Elizabeth Hollowell; three sisters, Sara Howard,
   Sara Hollowell, and Christian Oudelant. (The Chuckatuck
   Friends Records, p. 90)

20 da 2 mo 1693 - HOLLOWELL, Henry of Elizabeth River, and
   Elizabeth Scott of Nansemond County. (The Chuckatuck
   Friends Records, p.125)

14 December 1786 - HOLT, John and Angelica Eppes. Sur. Little-
   bury Hardyman. (Charles City Courthouse records)

30 December 1844 - HOOD, Thomas and Eliza Warren, by R. B.
   Foster. (Dinwiddie County D.B. 4, p. 768)

5 September 1792 - HOOE, Robert H. of Stafford County and
   Catharine Marshall. Sur. William Fauntleroy. (Marriages
   of Richmond County, Virginia 1668-1853 by George H. S.
   King)

__ March 1778 - HOPE, William and _____. (King and
   Queen County Licenses, Marriage and Ordinary - date as
   reported by clerk. The bride's name not shown)

17 January 1763 - HOPKINS, James of James City County, and
   Elizabeth Marston, spinster of this county. Sur. John
   Soane Marston of Charles City County; wit. James New.
   (Charles City County Marriage Licenses)

29 December 1813 - HORNER, Samuel and Catharine Cross, daughter
   of Joseph Cross of King and Queen County. Sur. Reuben

Cross. (Chesterfield County Marriage Register, p. 123)

14 March 1787 - HORSELEY, James Taylor and Johanna Dudley, Gloucester County. (Christ Church Parish Register, p. 265)

20 December 1787 - HORSLEY, Smith and Elizabeth Rilee, Gloucester County. (Christ Church Parish Register, p. 266)

23 May 1825 - HOSKINS, George W. and Sarah Jane Duke, both of Hanover County. (Rev. Talley's Register, p. 6)

3 July 1832 - HOTT, Lewis and Mary Ann Wright, both of Hanover. (Rev. Talley's Register, p. 17)

6 da 3 mo 1782 - HOUGH, Mahlon, son of John Hough of Loudoun County and Mary Stabler, daughter of Edward Stabler of Dinwiddie County, married at Fairfax. (Marriage Records Fairfax Monthly Meeting [Friends] 1760-1892, p. 78)

30 da 4 mo 1783 - HOUGH, Samuel, son of John Hough of Loudoun County, and Ann Stabler, daughter of Edward Stabler of Dinwiddie County, married at Fairfax. (Marriage Records Fairfax Monthly Meeting [Friends] 1760-1892, p. 80)

11 October 1660 - HOULDWORTH and Naomi Davis. (Virginia Colonial Abstracts, v.11, p. 92, Charles City County Order Book, p.270)

18 May 1836 - HOWARD, Richard H. and Mary Jane Harper, by Russel B. Foster. (Dinwiddie County D.B. 2, p. 517)

__ August 1778 - HOWELL, William and ____ ____. (King and Queen Licenses - Marriage and Ordinary. Date as reported by the clerk. Bride's name not shown)

28 July 1792 - HOWERTON, Philip and Susanna Smith, spinster, daughter of Henry Smith. Sur. William Smith. (Buckingham County Marriage Bond)

22 December 1825 - HOWLE, Gidion N. of New Kent County and Orina Gathright of Hanover County. (Rev. Talley's Register, p. 7)

21 December 1788 - HOWLETT, Nicholas and Elizabeth Halyard, King and Queen County. (Christ Church Parish Register, p. 194)

1 January 1835 - HOY, David F. and Elizabeth G. Elder, by Isham E. Hargrave. (Dinwiddie County D.B. 2, p. 37)

24 June 1847 - HOY, David F. and Elizabeth T. Elliott, by I. E. Hargrave. (Dinwiddie County D.B. 5, p. 578)

29 October 1845 - HOY, P. H. and Ann W. Clay, by J. W. Roper. (Dinwiddie County D.B. 5, p. 391)

21 December 1837 - HOY, Paton and Jane Richerson, by J. W. Roper. (Dinwiddie County D.B. 2, p. 255)

15 May 1823 - HUBBARD, Samuel and Hannah Hurt, both of Hanover County. (Rev. Talley's Register, p. 2)

23 August 1786 - HUDDLESTON, Simon and Lucy Page, daughter of

James Page who is Surety. (Buckingham Marriage Bonds)

20 October 1777 - 20 October 1778 - HUDGEN, Anthony and Sarah Hundley. (Gloucester County Licenses - Marriage and Ordinary. Date as reported by clerk)

8 February 1787 - HUDGINS, Holloway and Nancy Berryman, spinster of lawful age. Sur. Matthew Branch. (Buckingham County Marriage Bond)

15 December 1836 - HUDSON, Lewis and Emily F. Wesbrook, by Russel B. Foster. (Dinwiddie County D.B. 2, p. 517)

17 March 1835 - HUDSON, Theophilus and Martha Eckles, by Russel B. Foster. (Dinwiddie County D.B. 2, p. 517)

22 April 1792 - HUGGET, Thomas and Frances Ware, King and Queen County. (Christ Church Parish Register, p. 257)

13 June 1834 - HUGHES, Charles, bachelor and Miss Charity Wood, both of Hanover County. Married 19 June 1834 by Rev. Talley. (Hanover County Miscellany and Rev. Talley's Register, p. 20)

22 September 1840 - HUGHES, Harman, bachelor and Miss Mary Ellen Davis. (Hanover County Miscellany)

2 September 1824 - HUGHES, Henry and Agnes Wade, both of Hanover County. (Rev. Talley's Register, p. 3)

11 June 1784 - HUGHES, William and Sarah Harding. (Hanover County Licenses - Marriage and Ordinary. Date as reported by clerk)

6 May 1797 - HULETT, William and Lucy Roper. David Roper consents for "my ward". Sur. Barvel Sharp and wit. Peter West. (Charles City County Courthouse records)

26 November 1835 - HUNDLEY, Anthony S. and Winney Crowder, by W. Hyde. (Dinwiddie County D.B. 1, p. 417)

20 December 1842 - HUNDLEY, Nelson, bachelor, and Miss Sarah Wright. (Hanover County Miscellany)

18 May 1842 - HUNT, Henry G. and Susan H. Peterson, by Smith Parham. (Dinwiddie County D.B. 3, p. 478)

20 October 1777 - 20 October 1778 - HUNT, John and Mary Glass. (Gloucester County Licenses - Marriage and Ordinary. Date as reported by clerk)

3 November 1825 - HUNTER, John and Isabella Potty, Louisa County. (St. Martin's Parish Register, p. 29)

3 da 6 mo 1764 - HUTCHINS, Nicholas, son of Strangoman Hutchins of Goochland County, and Sarah Ladd, daughter of John Ladd, dec'd of Charles City County, at the Meeting House at Wainoak [sic]. (White Oak Swamp Friends Records, p. 217)

___ June 1778 - HUTSON, William and _____. (King and Queen Licenses - Marriage and Ordinary. Date as reported by clerk. Bride's name not shown)

About 1686 - IRBY, William Jr. of Charles City County, and Elizabeth Mascall, widow of Richard Mascall. (Marriages of Henrico County, Virginia 1680-1808 by Joyce Lindsay, p. 46)

8 January 1822 - IRBY, William Stuard and Flavilla Marston who consents. Sur. Giles Buffin. (Charles City County Court-House records)

12 February 1762 - IVERSON, Richard of Gloucester County, and Rebecca Dudley, widow of William Dudley, deceased. Sur. and wit. Robert Johnston and William Bickham. (Middlesex County Marriage Register, p. 13)

23 December 1757 - IVERSON, Thomas of Gloucester County, bachelor, and Jane Montague, spinster. Vincent Vass gives consent for Jane. Sur. and Wit. Robert Elliot, William Moulson, Jn. Psinstsoff, Phi. Montague, and John Davis. (Middlesex County Marriage Register, p. 10)

20 October 1777 - 20 October 1778 - IVERSON, Thomas and Elizabeth Clayton. (Gloucester County Licenses - Marriage and Ordinary. Date as reported by clerk)

11 April 1791 - JACKMAN, Robert and Salley Hillen, Gloucester County. (Christ Church Parish Register, p. 268)

16 December 1799 - JACKSON, Jeremiah and Nancy Bell, daughter of John Bell who consents. Sur. and wit. John P. Gordon and Edm'd Christian. (Charles City County Marriage License)

8 November 1810 - JACKSON, Joseph and Patsey Roach. Sur. John Williams Roach. (Charles City County Marriage Licenses)

17 November 1786 - JAMISON, John and Sarah Palmer, of full age. Elizabeth Palmer, mother of Sarah consents. Sur. William Johnson Berryman, (Buckingham County Marriage Bond)

24 June 1780 - JARRETT, Richard and Amey Stephens. Sur. John Harwood. (Charles City County Marriage License)

24 March 1835 - JARVIS, Collin of James City, widower, and Miss Mary White of Hanover County. Married 25 March 1835 by Rev. Charles Talley. (Hanover County Miscellany and Rev. Talley's Register, p. 22)

23 December 1771 - JEFFERSON, Thomas and Martha Skelton, widow, of Charles City County. Sur. Francis Eppes. (Colonial Papers, Folder 49, Item 5)

3 January 1785 - JENKINS, Levi and Mary Waddrop [Waldrop?]. Sur. and Wit. John Harwood and L. Bacon. (Charles City County Marriage License)

30 November 1830 - JERDONE, John and Barbary Ann Callis, Louisa County. (St. Martin's Parish Register, p. 29)

24 June 1780 - JERRET, Richard and Amy Stephens. Sur. John

Harwood. (Charles City County Marriage records, Box 9, V.S.L.)

17 March 1864 - JEWELL, John R. and Jane C. Hanes. (St. Martin's Parish Register, p. 33)

16 November 1844 - JINKINS, Absalom H., bachelor, and Miss Martha Tucker. (Hanover County Miscellany)

26 June 1845 - JINKINS, William B., bachelor, and Miss Caroline Franklin. (Hanover County Miscellany)

8 January 1851 - JOHNSON, Alexander and Sarah Ann Perkins, by I. E. Hargrave. (Dinwiddie County Marriage Book 1848-1867, p. 103)

22 November 1853 - JOHNSON, Andrew J. and Miss Catherine B. Harris. (St. Martin's Parish Register, p. 32)

14 February 1817 - JOHNSON, Bailey S. and Sarah L. White, both of Hanover County. (Hanover County Miscellany)

30 October 1838 - JOHNSON, Benjamin and Harriet Coalman, by J. W. Roper. (Dinwiddie County D.B. 2, p. 255)

20 November 1810 - JOHNSON, Edmund and Lucy Solomon. Nathaniel Martin of Prince George County guardian for Lucy and gives consent. Sur. Randolph Johnson. (Surry County Marriage Register, p. 84)

22 January 1839 - JOHNSON, Francis W. of Richmond, bachelor, and Miss Eliza Ann Mantlo of Hanover County. Married 24 January 1839 by Rev. Charles Talley. (Hanover Miscellany and Rev. Talley's Register, p. 26)

_____ 1836 - JOHNSON, Lewis of Richmond and Miss Judith C. Mantlo of Hanover County. (Rev. Talley's Register, p. 24)

25 July 1818 - JOHNSON, Moses and Dinah Butcher, by Chas. Roper. (Dinwiddie County Marriage Book 1849-1867, p. 104)

12 April 1834 - JOHNSON, Thomas of King William County and Miss Temperance Turner of Hanover. License obtained in Henrico County. (Rev. Talley's Register, p. 20)

29 August 1788 - JOHNSON, William, Esq. and Mary Cobbs, spinster. Witnesses: Samuel Hill, James Smith, and John Massie. Marriage Agreement recorded 2 April 1789. (Hanover County Court Records 1783-1792)

14 December 1780 - JOHNSON, William and Dorothea Thomas. (Hanover County Licenses - Marriage and Ordinary. Date as reported by clerk.

29 December 1831 - JOLLY, Archibald and Elizabeth Perkins, by John Grammer, Jr. (Dinwiddie County D.B. 1, p. 244)

_____ October 1826 - JONES, Albert and Catharine Boaze. (Rev. Talley's Register, p. 9)

13 December 1837 - JONES, Albert S. and Miss Frances Clopton, both of Hanover County. (Rev. Talley's Register, p. 25)

6 September 1793 - JONES, Drury of Dinwiddie County and Mary
   Simmons, daughter of Martha Feild. Sur. Gale Lewis. (Brunswick County Marriage Register, p. 77)

10 August 1832 - JONES, Francis D. of Gloucester County, and
   Lucy Jones Peck. Sur. Harriot Peck. (Marriages of
   Richmond County, Virginia 1668-1853 by George H. S. King)

24 February 1841 - JONES, Henry M. and Mary Williamson, by
   J. W. Roper. (Dinwiddie County D.B. 3, p. 565)

7 May 1784 - JONES, John and Prudence Hazelwood, daughter of
   Mary Hazelwood of Hanover County who consents. Wit. Hugh
   Mosely. (Marriages of Henrico County, Virginia 1680-1808
   by Joyce Lindsay, p. 49)

25 August 1835 - JONES, John A., bachelor, and Miss Ann Wyatt
   Mills, both of Hanover County. Married 10 September 1835
   by Rev. Talley. (Hanover County Miscellany and Rev.
   Talley's Register, p. 23)

31 January 1769 - JONES, JOhn, Jr. of Dinwiddie County, and
   Elizabeth Crawley, daughter of William Crawley, Gent.,
   of Amelia County who consents. Sur. Thos. Jones. (Amelia
   County Marriage Register, p. J-1)

29 December 1836 - JONES, Philip B. and Miss Elizabeth T. A.
   Sutton. (St. Martin's Parish Register, p. 30)

12 February ____ - JONES, Philip Greenhill and Sarah Cox, by
   Russel B. Foster. (Dinwiddie County D.B. 3, p. 609)

27 December 1837 - JONES, Richard Williams of Richmond, and
   Levenia B. Meredith of Hanover County. (Rev. Talley's
   Register, p. 25)

10 da 5 mo 1683 - JONES, Robart and Martha Rice of Nansemond
   County. (The Chuckatuck Friends Records, p. 117)

21 May 1834 - JONES, Robert H. and Martha E. F. Boisseau,
   by I. E. Hargrave. (Dinwiddie County D.B. 1, p. 195)

23 August 1788 - JONES, Thomas and Elizabeth Didlake, King and
   Queen County. (Christ Church Parish Register, p. 266)

29 December 1838 - JONES, Thomas A. and Mary Ann King, by I. E.
   Hargrave. (Dinwiddie County D.B. 2, p. 529)

8 July 1686 - JONES, William of New Kent County and Alice Lee
   of this parish. (Christ Church Parish Register, p. 29)

__ December 1776 - JONES, William and Elizabeth Roberts. (James
   City Licenses - Marriage and Ordinary. Date as reported
   by clerk)

29 December 1836 - JONES, William A. and Miss Mary Via, both
   of Hanover County. (Rev. Talley's Register, p. 24)

2 June 1835 - JONES, William B. and Elizabeth B. Jones, by
   Russel B. Foster. (Dinwiddie County D.B. 2, p. 517)

17 May 1832 - JONES, William G. and Miss Nancy G. Branch, by
   W. J. Plumer. (Dinwiddie County D.B. 1, p. 90)

29 da 3 mo 1688 - JORDAN, James, son of Thomas of County of
Nanzemund and Eliza Ratliff, daughter of Richard Ratliff
of Isle of Wight County. Among the witnesses: father,
Tho: Jordan; mother, Margaret Jordan; cuzen [sic], Tho.
Davis; duzen [sic] John Newell. (The Chuckatuck Friends
Records, p. 69)

9 da 12 mo 1688 - JORDAN, John, son of Thomas Jordan of Nanse-
mund County, and Margaret Burgh of ye same place, married
in "ye house of his father." Among the witnesses: father,
Thomas Jordan; mother, Margaret Jordan; ouncle [sic], John
Brassere; bro. Tho. Jordan, Jun.; bro., Robard Jordan;
ouncle [sic] James Davis; ante [sic] Abigail Brassere;
sister, Elizabeth Jordan; ante [sic] Margaret Davis; sister, Christian Jordan. (The Chuckatuck Friends Records,
p. 66)

6 da 7 mo 1699 - JORDAN, Mathew, the son of Thomas Jordan of
Chuckatuck and Dorrithy Bufkin, widdo [sic] woman, both of
Nansemond. Among the witnesses: father, Thomas Jordan;
Bros. Robart Jordan, Richard Jordan, Benjamine Jordan,
Samuel Jordan, Joshua Jordan; mother, Margaret Jordan;
Sisters, Elizabeth Jordan and Margaret Jordan. (The
Chuckatuck Friends Records, p. 135)

17 da 3 mo 1702 - JORDAN, Mathew of Nansemond County, and
Susanna Bresy, widow of Isle of Wight County. (The Chuckatuck Records, p. 140)

22 da 6 mo 1706 - JORDAN, Richard, son of Thomas Jordan of
Chuckatuck dec'd and Rebecca Rattcliff, daughter of Richard
Rattcliff of the Trerasco Necks, married in house of
Richard Rattcliff. Among witnesses: father, Richard
Rattcliff; bros. Benjamin Jordan, John Jordan, Robt. Jordan,
Joshua Jordan, James Jordan, Richard Rattcliff, and John
Rattcliff; mother, Elizabeth Rattcliff and mother,
Margaret Jordan. (The Chuckatuck Friends Records, p. 146)

9 da 12 mo 1687 - JORDAN, Robert, son of Tho: Jordan of Nanze-
mund, and Christian Oudeland "ye daughter of Tho. Taberer
of Isle of Wight County. Among the witnesses: father,
Thomas Jordan; mother, Margaret Jordan; ouncle, John Bras-
ser; bro., Thomas Jordan, Junr.; ouncle, James Davis; bro.
John Jordan; ante [sic], Abagail Brasser; sister, Eliza
Jordan; ante [sic], Margaret Davis; sister, Christian
Jordan. (The Chuckatuck Friends Records, p. 67)

10 da 5 mo 1690 - JORDAN, Robert, son of Thos. Jordan of
Chuckatuck in ye County of Nanzemund, and MaryBelson,
daughter of Edmond Belson, dec'd of Nanzemun, married in
John Scott's house. Among the witnesses: father, Thos.
Jordan; mother, Margaret Jordan; bros. Edmond Belson,
Thos. Jordan, John Jordan, James Jordan, John Scott; sis-
ters, Elizabeth Scott, Elizabeth Jordan, and Margaret
Jordan. (The Chuckatuck Friends Records, p. 128)

11 da 1 mo 1764 - JORDAN, Robert, son of Benjamin Jordan and
Lydia Jordan of Henrico County, and Mary Ellyson of New
Kent County, daughter of Joseph Ellyson and Mary Ellyson.
Married at Black Creek Meeting House in New Kent. (White
Oak Swamp Friends Records, p. 87)

6 da 10 mo 1679 - JORDAN, Thomas, son of Thos. Jordan of

Nansemun and Elizabeth Burgh, daughter of William Burgh, deceased. Among the witnesses: father, Thos. Jordan; mother, Margaret Jordan; her brother, Georg Billingsly; his three brothers, John Jordan, James Jordan and Robert Jordan; her sister, Moarning Burgh. (The Chuckatuck Friends Records, p. 87)

14 da 7 mo 1701 - JORDWIN, James and Anne Roseter of Elizabeth River "took each other in marriage." (The Chuckatuck Friends Records, p. 139)

K

19 September 1850 - KEAN, Napolean B. and Miss Lucy A. S. Harris. (St. Martin's Parish Register, p. 32)

5 November 1819 - KEESEE, Thomas and Nancy F. Sharpe, who consents. Sur. Edward Folkes. (Charles City Courthouse records)

6 March 1791 - KEININGHAM, Benjamin and Rose Berryman Shackelford, King and Queen County. (Christ Church Parish Register, p. 268)

22 August 1793 - KEITH, John and Mary Holden Taliaferro, King and Queen County. (Christ Church Parish Register, p. 116)

19 August 1826 - KENDRICK, Robert and Frances Watkins, both of Hanover. (Rev. Talley's Register, p. 8)

12 September 1816 - KENDRICK, Thornton S., bachelor, and Miss Martha Elmore. (Hanover County Miscellany)

__ March 1782 - KENINGHAM, William and Caty [Killigrew?], Gloucester County. (Christ Church Parish Register, p. 269)

9 September 1840 - KENT, Robert, bachelor, and Miss Lucretia Martin. (Hanover County Miscellany)

22 August 1793 - KEITH, _____, and Mary Holden Taliaferro, King and Queen County. (Christ Church Parish Register, p. 257)

8 August 1771 - KER, David of King and Queen County and Frances Tucker. (Christ Church Parish Register, p. 303)

30 December 1845 - KERBY, Edward, bachelor, and Miss Mary Martin. (Hanover County Miscellany)

20 June 1843 - KERBY, Henry, bachelor, and Miss Edy Martin. (Hanover County Miscellany)

27 December 1823 - KERSEY, Edward and Jane Tate, both of Hanover County. (Rev. Talley's Register, p. 3)

13 June 1824 - KERSEY, Matthew and Rebecca Hancock, both of Hanover County. (Rev. Talley's Register, p. 3)

26 May 1831 - KERSEY, William and Belle Bailey, both of Hanover (Rev. Talley's Register, p. 15)

25 December 1823 - KEY, John and Susanna Harris, people of color. (Rev. Talley's Register, p. 2)

25 January 1844 - KEYS, Lemuel and Polly Gray, by I. E. Hargrave. (Dinwiddie County, D.B. 4, p. 407)

31 January 1844 - KIDD, William R. and Martha F. Young, by J. W. Roper. (Dinwiddie County D.B. 5, p. 390)

23 September 1847 - KING, Peter and Martha E. L. Eckles, by Russel B. Foster. (Dinwiddie County Marriage Book 1849-1867, p.102)

14 April 1827 - KIRBY, Garland and Polley Burnett, both of Hanover (Rev. Talley's Register, p. 9)

20 February 1851 - KIRKS, William H. and Elizabeth P. Sandifer, by F. A.Gossee. (Dinwiddie County Marriage Book 1849-1867, p.106)

29 December 1786 - KIDD, Absolom and Lettice Owen, of full age. Sur. Jesse Kidd. (Buckingham County Marriage Bond)

8 January 1784 - KIDD, Benjamin and Mary Guthrie, King and Queen County. (Christ Church Parish Register, p. 263)

8 August 1660 - KIGAN, Dennis and Phebie Banks. (VCA 11, Charles City County, p. 92, Order Book, p. 270)

__ June 1715 - KNIGHT, John of Stafford County and Katherine Phillips. (Marriages of Richmond County, Virginia 1668-1853 by George H. S. King, p. 114)

21 October 1695 - KNOX, Jno. and Winifrid Cormer. (Elizabeth City County Deeds and Wills 1684,1688, and 1702, p. 168)

1 December 1775 - 1 January 1778 - KYLE, David and Elizabeth Chambers. (Buckingham County Licenses - Marriage and Ordinary. Date as reported by clerk)

L

22 January 1787 - LACY, Henry and Lucy Duke Timberlake, ward of Henry Duke who consents. Sur. John Timberlake. (Charles City County Licenses)

15 September 1791 - LACY, Isaac and Elizabeth Walker. (Charles City County, Virginia Magazine of History and Biography, v. 23, p. 87)

11 da 8 mo 1763 - LADD, Amos, son of John Ladd, dec'd of Charles City County, and Sarah Binford, daughter of Thomas Binford, dec'd of Henrico County. (White Oak Swamp Friends Records, p. 82)

10 da 9 mo 1767 - LADD, Joseph, won of John Ladd, dec'd of New Kent County, and Mary Binford, daughter of Thomas Binford, dec'd of Henrico County. (White Oak Swamp Friends Records, p. 140)

15 da 6 mo 1807 - LADD, Robert, son of William Ladd, dec'd of Charles City County, and Mary Terrell, daughter of [mutilated] Terrell, dec'd of Caroline County. (Cedar Creek Friends Records, Marriage Certificates 1799-1808)

8 da 12 mo 1761 - LADD, Thomas, son of William Ladd of Charles

City County, dec'd, and Ann Ellyson, daughter of Thomas Ellyson of Chesterfield County, dec'd. (White Oak Swamp Friends Records, p. 66)

26 November 1770 - LAMB, John and Fanny Finch, daughter of William Finch. Consent only. (Charles City Courthouse records)

18 October 1786 - LAMBETH, Thomas and Lucy Kidd, King and Queen County. (Christ Church Parish Register, p. 265)

23 December 1858 - LANE, George W. and Edmonia E. Thacker. (St. Martin's Parish Register, p. 33)

2 May 1843 - LANIER, Don S. and Sarah F. Prosise, by I. E. Hargrave. (Dinwiddie County D.B. 4, p. 407)

6 November 1850 - LANIER, John T. and Martha D. Sturdivant, by I. E. Hargrave. (Dinwiddie County Marriage Book 1849-1867, p. 103)

19 February 1835 - LANIER, Lewis P. and Elizabeth F. Sturdivant, by I. E. Hargrave. (Dinwiddie County, D.B. 1,p. 373)

22 February 1848 - LAWRENCE, George and Miss M. R. Vaughan. (St. Martin's Parish Register, p. 32)

12 June 1786 - LAX, Elisha and Mary Neighbors, of full age. Sur. William Phelps. (Buckingham County Marriage Bond)

4 November 1852 - LEADBETTER, William H. and Susan A. L. Evans, by I. E. Hargrave. (Dinwiddie County Marriage Book 1849-1867, p. 109)

24 October 1850 - LEE, Benjamin E. and Lucy A. Wells, by I. E. Hargrave. (Dinwiddie County Marriage Book 1849-1867, p.103)

1 December 1753 - LEE, Henry and Lucy Grimes, daughter of Charles Grimes, Esq. of Richmond County. Married in James City Parish, James City County by the Rev. Mr. William Preston. (Marriages of Richmond County, Virginia, 1668-1853 by George H. S. King, p. 116)

23 December 1841 - LEE, Henry and Mary B. E. Young, by T. T. Castleman. (Dinwiddie County D.B. 4, p. 126)

1 December 1775 - 1 January 1778 - LEE, Young and Jamima Matthews. (Buckingham County Licenses - Marriage and Ordinary. Date as reported by clerk)

15 April 1781 - LeFRANCE, John and Jane Bolling Kenny. Sur. and Wit. James Boisseau and James New. (Charles City County License)

— November 1782 - LENNARD, Samuel and Anne Thompson, spinster, daughter of Mary Tomson who consents and calls her "Nancy." Sur. John Hilliard. (Charles City County Marriages, Box 9, V.S.L.)

24 February 1812 - LEWELLIN, Moise and Polly Ward, spinster, Sur. and Wit. Thomas Ware, Thos. Grant, Sarah Ware, and William Gregory. (King William County Marriage Contract,

Book 6, p. 101. The date is that of the contract)

26 October 1842 - LEWIS, Albert W. and Ann G. Richerson, by
J. W. Roper. (Dinwiddie County D.B. 3, p. 565)

22 December 1842 - LEWIS, Devereux and Susan Abernathy, by I. E.
Hargrave. (Dinwiddie County D.B. 4, p. 407)

11 August 1846 - LEWIS, Edwin and Susan R. Thrift, by I. E.
Hargrave. (Dinwiddie County D.B. 5, p. 295)

14 December 1836 - LEWIS, Francis P. and Elizabeth Chambers, by
J. W. Roper. (Dinwiddie County D.B. 2, p. 255)

___ June 1845 - LEWIS, George W. and Louisa Abernathy, by J. W.
Roper. (Dinwiddie County D.B. 5, p. 391)

18 March 1850 - LEWIS, Hamlin and Antoinette Wells, by I. E.
Hargrave. (Dinwiddie County Marriage Book 1849-1867, p.100)

1 June 1846 - LEWIS, Henry C. and Martha Harriet Wells, by I. E.
Hargrave. (Dinwiddie County D.B. 5, p. 295)

24 October 1681 - LEWIS, John of New Kent County and Elizabeth
O. Brissell (?). (Christ Church Parish Register, p. 17)

12 December 1844 - LEWIS, John Dr. and Miss Barbara J. Winston.
(St. Martin's Parish Register, p. 30)

22 October 1848 - LEWIS, John B. and Mary J. Wells, by I. E.
Hargrave. (Dinwiddie County D.B. 6, p. 191)

23 October 1845 - LEWIS, Joseph and Julia C. Spain, by R. B.
Foster. (Dinwiddie County D.B. 4, p. 768)

14 June 1787 - LEWIS, Nicholas and Joice Shepard, Gloucester
County. (Christ Church Parish Register, p. 193)

24 June 1836 - LEWIS, Richard and Celia Abernathy, by I. E.
Hargrave. (Dinwiddie County D.B. 2, p. 37)

20 December 1849 - LEWIS, Richard S. and Henrietta S. Williamson, by J. W. Roper. (Dinwiddie County Marriage Book
1849-1867, p. 102)

30 October 1834 - LEWIS, Robert A. and Mary Ann Lewis, by I. E.
Hargrave. (Dinwiddie County D.B. 1, p. 195)

23 December 1842 - LEWIS, Thomas and Martha Lewis, by I. E.
Hargrave. (Dinwiddie County D.B. 4, p. 407)

15 December 1835 - LEWIS, William H. and Catharine E. Clay, by
I. E. Hargrave. (Dinwiddie County D. B. 1, p. 373)

15 October 1851 - LEWIS, William M. and Amy E. Boisseau, by
I. E. Hargrave. (Dinwiddie County Marriage Book 1849-
1867, p.106)

22 December 1824 - LIGGON, Henry F. and Nancy Ann Wade. (Rev.
Talley's Register, p. 4)

13 January 1762 - LIGHTFOOT, Sherwood and Elizabeth Brewer (?).
Sur. and Wit. Brazure Williams, James New, and Nath'l

MAYNARD.   (Charles City Marriage License)

3 November 1792 - LIPSCOMB, Daniel of St. John's Parish, King
    William County, and Jane Frazer, daughter of Jane Lipscomb.
    Wit. Wm. Alvey, Sr., Benoni Lipscomb, and Ambrose Lips-
    comb. Date is that of marriage contract. (King William
    County Record Book 3, p. 1)

26 October 1785 - LIPSCOMB, George of St. John's Parish, and
    Ann Lipscomb of same Parish. Wit. John Pemberton, Martin
    Slaughter, and Wilson C. Pember. (King William County
    Record Book 2, pp. 63-68. Marriage Contract. Date is
    that of contract)

24 January 1827 - LIPSCOMB, Nicholas and Virginia Batkins.
    License obtained in Hanover. (Rev. Talley's Register, p. 9)

30 November 1830 - LIPSCOMB, Roscoe and Jane Maria Dejarnet.
    (St. Martin's Parish Register, p. 29)

30 June 1825 - LITTLEPAGE, Francis and Catharine Durham, both
    of Hanover County. (Rev. Talley's Register, p. 6)

16 January 1834 - LIVESAY, George W. of Franklin County, and
    Orina F. McGhee of Hanover. Married by Rev. Charles Talley.
    (Hanover County Miscellany and Rev. Talley's Register,
    p.19)

4 December 1801 - LIVESAY, Peter and Susanna McGhee, daughter of
    John McGhee of Hanover County who consents. Sur. and Wit.
    Joseph McGhee and Elizabeth Lewis. (Marriages of Henrico
    County, Virginia 1680-1808 by Joyce Lindsay, p. 54)

8 January 1694/5 - LONG, William and Jane Proby. (Elizabeth
    City County, Deeds and Wills 1684,1688, and 1702, p. 168)

8 April 1851 - LOWRY, James W. and Miss Sarah G. Perkins. (St.
    Martin's Parish Register, p. 32)

28 April 1829 - LOWERY, Richard E. and Eliza Ann Gentry. (St.
    Martin's Parish Register, p. 29)

15 April 1846 - LOWRY, Thos. C. and Miss Lucy Mason. (St.
    Martin's Parish Register, p. 32)

29 December 1824 - LOWERY, Wilson and Mary A. Perkins. (St.
    Martin's Parish Register, p. 29)

22 December 1824 - LOYD, George and Ann Eshon, who consents.
    Sur. and Wit. George B. Lacy and R. F. Graves. (Charles
    City County Marriage Licenses)

26 December 1848 - LUCK, William H. and Miss Susan Page. (St.
    Martin's Parish Register, p. 32)

22 August 1850 - LUCY, George H. and Martha Ann Spicely, by
    John G. Claiborne, (Dinwiddie County Marriage Book 1849-
    1867, p. 101)

7 January 1792 - LUMPKIN, Coleman and Sarah Calaun, Gloucester
    County. (Christ Church Parish Register, p. 197)

22 December 1791 - LUMPKIN, Robert, Jr. and Lucy Roane, King

and Queen County. (Christ Church Parish Register, p. 197)

3 October 1848 - LUNSFORD, David A. and Mary E. Grigg, by Russel
    B. Foster. (Dinwiddie County Marriage Book 1849-1867,
    p. 102)

11 December 1823 - LYLE, Daniel and Catharine Cross, both of
    Hanover County. (Rev. Talley's Register, p. 2)

17 February 1781 - LYSAUGHT, John and Sarah Tyler. (Hanover
    County Licenses - Marriage and Ordinary. Date as reported
    by clerk)

Mc

7 September 1791 - McCORMACK, Thomas and Mary Taylor, daughter
    of Daniel Taylor who consents and is Surety. (Buckingham
    County Marriage Bond)

4 September 1828 - McGHEE, John C. and Miss Caroline Hazelgrove,
    both of Hanover County. (Rev. Talley's Register, p. 11)

6 September 1844 - McGREGOR, Allen W., bachelor and Miss Sarah
    Martin. (Hanover County Miscellany)

15 January 1828 - McKINNEY, Collier and Mary Spraggin. Sur.
    John Blaxten. (Charles City County Courthouse records)

8 July 1829 - McKINNEY, William and Eleanor Pointer. William
    Tyler, guardian of Eleanor and who consents. Sur. Edward
    Adams. (Charles City Marriage Licenses)

3 August 1784 - McWILLIAMS, Benjamin and Letitia Brown, widow,
    who consents. Sur. John Colgin. (Charles City County
    Marriage Licenses, Box 9, V.S.L.)

20 January 1787 - McWILLIAMS, John and Elizabeth Green, King
    and Queen County. (Christ Church Parish Register, p. 265)

M

25 January 1814 - MACHEN, Henry of Prince George County, and
    Nancy Wilkinson, twenty-one years of age. Sur. Richard
    Wilkinson. (Marriages of Chesterfield County, Virginia by
    Catherine Knorr, p. 81)

28 September 1783 - MACKENDREE, John and Ruthey Milby, King
    and Queen County. (Christ Church Parish Register, p. 263)

14 February 1848 - MADDOX, Robert and Lucy Waddill, daughter of
    Mary Waddill. Lucy signs consents. Sur. and Wit. John F.
    Southall. (Charles City County Licenses)

26 January 1832 - MAHONE, James J. of Henrico County, and
    Lurancy Barker of Hanover County. (Rev. Talley's Register,
    p. 16)

29 February 1844 - MAITLAND, James and Mary Wells, by I. E.
    Hargrave. (Dinwiddie County D.B. 4, p. 407)

4 September 1839 - MALLORY, John N. and Elizabeth Page. (St.
    Martin's Parish Register, p. 30)

29 July 1852 - MALLORY, Joseph S. and Miss Arabella V. Lane. (St. Martin's Parish Register, p. 32)

9 October 1851 - MALLROY, Otho A. and Miss Mary W. Hott. (St. Martin's Parish Register, p. 32)

17 July 1833 - MALONE, William and Charlotte Johnson, by R. B. FOSTER. (Dinwiddie County D. B. 1, p. 298)

6 February 1823 - MANTLO, George and Judith O. Skelton, both of Hanover. (Rev. Talley's Register, p. 1)

5 February 1823 - MANTLO, Hezekiah and Elizabeth Wade, both of Hanover County. (Rev. Talley's Register, p. 1)

22 December 1812 - MARRABLE, Abraham and Judy Loyd. Sur. and Wit. John Blaton and Ro. W. Christian. (Charles City County Marriage Licenses, Box 9, V.S.L.)

1 January 1772 - MARRABLE, William and Susannah Weaver, spinster, daughter of Joseph Weaver. Marston Williams gives oath that Susanna is of full age. (Charles City County, Virginia Magazine of History and Biography, v. 23, p. 87)

5 February 1778 - MARSH, Aaron and Mary Boaz. (Hanover County Licenses - Marriage and Ordinary. Date as reported by clerk)

15 July 1867 - MARSHALL, John Mr. of Fauquier County and Miss Millie Jones, sister of H. P. Jones, Esq., Hanover Academy. (St. Martin's Parish Register, p. 33)

15 November 1827 - MARSTON, John T. and Frances B. Parker, who consents. Sur. Albert Hankins. (Charles City County Marriage Licenses)

19 December 1845 - MARTIN, Bartholomew, bachelor, and Miss Sarah Wright. (Hanover County Miscellany)

24 November 1840 - MARTIN, Charles, bachelor, and Miss Elizabeth Martin. (Hanover County Miscellany)

24 November 1832 - MARTIN, Ellyson and Ann Adams, both of Hanover County. (Rev. Talley's Register, p. 18)

23 May 1840 - MARTIN, George of Petersburg, and Jane Jones, daughter of John Jones. (Virginia Marriage Bonds, Richmond City, by Anne Waller Reddy and Andrew Lewis Riffe, IV, p. 71)

8 December 1831 - MARTIN, Gideon and Emeline Adams, both of Hanover. (Rev. Talley's Register, p. 16)

11 February 1828 - MARTIN, Parke and Patsey Wade, both of New Kent County. (Rev. Talley's Register, p. 10)

23 August 1837 - MARTIN, Robin and Mary Kerby, both of Hanover County. (Rev. Talley's Register, p. 25)

8 June 1787 - MARTIN, Joseph and Magdaline Lutterel. Sur. Presley Lutterel. (Buckingham County Marriage Bonds)

7 February 1834 - MARTIN, Josiah, bachelor, of New Kent County,

and Miss Mary Hollins of Hanover. Married 22 February 1834 by Rev. Talley. (Hanover Miscellany and Rev. Talley's Register, p. 19)

14 December 1826 - MARTIN, Thomas and Sarah Parsons. (Rev. Talley's Register, p. 9)

9 November 1830 - MARTIN, Thompson and Miss Melissa Talley, both of Hanover County. (Rev. Talley's Register, p. 13)

1 August 1844 - MARTIN, William, bachelor, and Miss Susan Kerby, (Hanover County Miscellany)

20 November 1850 - MARTIN, William and Miss Virginia H. Newbill, by W. E. Webb. (Dinwiddie County Marriage Book 1849-1867, p. 104)

18 May 1844 - MARTIN, William T. and Miss Sarah Adams. (Hanover County Miscellany)

25 December 1828 - MATTHEWS, Johnson and Catharine Martin, both of Hanover. (Rev. Talley's Register, p. 11)

9 February 1788 - MATTHIS, Thomas and Rebecca Moody, who consents. Sur. Thomas Moody. (Charles City County Licenses)

18 October 1808 - MAY, John Fitzhugh of Petersburg, Dinwiddie County, and Margaret B. Field. Sur. Thomas Simmons. Married 19 October by Rev. Wright Tucker. (Marriages of Brunswick County, Virginia by Catharine Knorr, p.62)

18 October 1832 - MAYES, Abraham and Ann H. Jackson, by I. E. Hargrave. (Dinwiddie County Marriage Book 1849-1867, p. 105)

6 November 1851 - MAYES, Daniel J. and Ellen A. A. Hardaway, by I. E. Hargrave. (Dinwiddie County Marriage Book 1849-1867, p. 106)

6 September 1848 - MAYES, Edward L. and Mary A. Hawks, by F. A. Gossee. (Dinwiddie County D.B. 6, p. 75)

25 May 1835 - MAYES, Joshua and Frances V. Eanes, by Russel B. Foster. (Dinwiddie County D.B. 2, p. 517)

12 August 1846 - MAYES, Stephen and Susan A. Lewis, by I. E. Hargrave. (Dinwiddie County D. B. 5, p. 295)

18 December 1834 - MAYES, Stephen M. and Judith P. Sturdivant, by I. E.Hargrave. (Dinwiddie County D. B. 1, p. 195)

27 May 1791 - MAYNARD, Crawley and Elizabeth Merry, daughter of David Merry who consents. Sur. Wm. Roane; wit. Robert Munford and Otway Byrd. (Charles City County Licenses)

21 December 1789 - MAYNARD, Nathaniel and Elizabeth Matthews. Sur. Thomas Matthews, Jr. (Charles City County Licenses)

18 September 1772 - MEADE, Andrew of Nansemond County, brother of David Meade of Nansemond County, and Susanna Stith, daughter of Buckner Stith. Sur. Francis Young. (Brunswick County Marriage Register, p. 11)

19 September 1842 - MEDLIN, Archibald and Matilda Hawkins, by
I. E. Hargrave. (Dinwiddie County D.B. 4, p. 407)

1 March 1836 - MELTON, Allen and Miss Frances McDougle, both of
Hanover County (Rev. Talley's Register, p. 24)

27 June 1838 - MELTON, Edward T., bachelor, and Miss Martha Ann
Tucker, both of Hanover County. (Rev. Talley's Register,
p. 26)

27 November 1845 - MEMS, William M. and Mary Crow, by J. W.
Roper. (Dinwiddie County D. B. 5, p. 391)

14 December 1836 - MEREDITH, Charles W. and Mary T. Chambers, by
J. W. Roper. (Dinwiddie County D. B. 2, p. 255)

21 December 1781 - MEREDITH, John of Dinwiddie County and Elizabeth Pennington. Sur. Frederick Pennington. (Sussex County Marriage Register, p. 29)

11 da 4 mo 1696 - MERRIDETH, Joseph, son of Samson Merideth of
Nansemond County, and Sara Denson, daughter of Frances
Denson of Isle of Wight County. (The Chuckatuck Friends
Records, p. 131)

10 February 1842 - MEREDITH, Robt. E. and Caroline Barnes, by
I. E. Hargrave. (Dinwiddie County D. B. 4, p. 407)

20 March 1845 - MEREDITH, Reuben C. Dr. and Lucy Ann Doswell.
(St. Martin's Parish Register, p. 30)

4 March 1847 - MEREDITH, Robert and Indiana L. Harris, Louisa
County. (St. Martin's Parish Register, p. 32)

30 April 1782 - MEREDITH, William and Judith Edmondson, King
and Queen County. (Christ Church Parish Register, p. 269)

8 da 4 mo 1759 - MERRIMOON, Peter, son of John Merrimon of
Amelia County, and Obedience Reams, daughter of William
Reams of Dinwiddie County. (White Oak Swamp Friends
Records, p. 28)

24 November 1835 - MESSENGER, Francis C. of Richmond, and Miss
Mildred A. Frazer of Hanover County. Married 3 December
1835 by Rev. Talley. (Hanover County Miscellany and Rev.
Talley's Register, p.23)

2 March 1826 - METTERT, Washington of Richmond and Emily J.
Bowles of Hanover County. (Rev. Talley's Register, p. 8)

10 November 1763 - MICHEL, Achelius and _____, daughter of
John Gregory who consents. (Charles City County Marriage
Licenses, consent only)

21 December 1841 - MILES, Benjamin and Martha A. Clay, by I. E.
Hargrave. (Dinwiddie County D.B. 4, p. 407)

5 January 1848 - MILES, Isham B. and Martha Ann Peeble, by
I. E. Hargrave. (Dinwiddie County, D.B. 5, p. 578)

3 May 1784 - MILES, James and Mary Thompson, who consents.
Sur. and wit. James Phillips and Peter Royster. (Charles
City County Marriages)

20 May 1820 - MILL, John and Frances Littlepage. Sur. James B. Littlepage. (King William County, Book 8, p. 156)

19 December 1780 - MILLS, Francis and Agnes Mills. (Hanover County Licenses, marriage and ordinary. Date as reported by the clerk)

19 October 1848 - MINETREE, Robert and Elizabeth Lewis. (Dinwiddie County D.B. 6, p. 191)

23 December 1835 - MINGGE, James J. and Nancy Poarch, by I. E. Hargrave. (Dinwiddie County D.B. 1, p. 373)

17 July 1848 - MINGGY, Robert and Mary Wynn, by F. A. Gossee. (Dinwiddie County D. B. 6, p. 75)

29 June 1793 - MINIE, Richard and Frances Leigh, King and Queen County. (Christ Church Parish Register, p. 257)

18 October 1786 - MINOR, Peter of Dinwiddie County and Hannah Jones, daughter of Peter Jones. Sur. Peter Jones. (Brunswick County Marriage Register, p. 41)

20 October 1777 - 20 October 1778 - MINOR, Thomas, Jr. and Ann Dawson. (Gloucester County Licenses - marriage and Ordinary. Date as reported by clerk)

28 January 1797 - MINSON, John and Ann Whitlock Wills, Sur. and wit. John Wills and Daniel Millar. (Charles City County Marriages)

4 August 1697 - MINSON, William and Easter Perrin. (Elizabeth City Deeds and Wills, 1684, 1688, and 1702, p. 168)

27 November 1763 - MITCHELL, Archelus and Mary Gregory, spinster, daughter of John Gregory. (Charles City County, William and Mary Quarterly, v.8, p. 196)

28 August 1754 - MITCHELL, Cary of Elizabeth City County and Martha Kello. Sur. and Wit. William Wager of James City County and R. Kello. (Southampton County Marriage Register, p. 2)

3 November 1830 - MITCHELL, Charles C. and Emily Brown. (St. Martin's Parish Register, p. 29)

30 June 1785 - MITCHELL, John and Sally Gatewood, King and Queen County. (Christ Church Parish Register, p. 264)

17 December 1846 - MITCHELL, John J. and Mrs. Mary Ann Spencer, by George A. Bain. (Dinwiddie County D. B. 5, p. 406)

2 December 1840 - MONTGOMERY, John and Miss Lucy Terrell. (St. Martin's Parish Register, p. 30)

19 December 1833 - MOODY, China and Elizabeth Sandifer, by I. E. Hargrave. (Dinwiddie County D. B. 1, p. 195)

7 January 1852 - MOODY, Samuel W. and Adelia A. Perkinson, by Hosea Crowder. (Dinwiddie County Marriage Book 1849-1867, p. 107)

19 December 1782 - MOORE, Benjamin and Susanna Milbey of King

and Queen County. (Christ Church Parish Register, p. 262)

2 May 1788 - MOORE, Bernard of King William County and Lucy
Leiper, niece of And. Leiper who consents and is surety.
(Marriages of Henrico County, Virginia 1680-1808 by Joyce
H. Lindsay, p. 60)

30 October 1850 - MOORE, Lemuel and Miss Pamelia D. Mallory.
(St. Martin's Parish Register, p. 32)

9 September 1840 - MOORE, William F. and Rebecca A. J. Bishop,
by I. E. Hargrave. (Dinwiddie County D. B. 3, p. 96)

23 January 1823 - MORECOCK, Wm. B. and Ann C. Edloe, who consents. Sur. John Armistead. (Charles City County Marriage
Licenses)

28 July 1828 - MORGAN, Joshiah of Gloucester County and Malvina
Weathers, daughter of Rebecca Weathers who consents. Sur.
William Morgan. (Marriages of Richmond County, Virginia
1668-1853, by George H. S. King, p. 138)

12 October 1854 - MORRIS, Charles and Miss Mary M. Morris,
Goochland County. (St. Martin's Parish Register, p. 32)

29 November 1849 - MOSBY, James R. and Miss Eliza A. Perkins.
(St. Martin's Parish Register, p. 32)

21 February 1787 - MOSS, Thomas and Betsey Toney, spinster.
Sur. William Toney. (Buckingham County Marriage Bonds)

6 December 1782 - MOULSON, William and Ann Guthrie of King and
Queen County. (Christ Church Parish Register, p. 262)

15 November 1828 - MOUNTCASTLE, Joseph T. and Mildred Snips.
Sur and Wit. Thomas B. New and Jas. P. Apperson. (Charles
City County Marriage Licenses)

2 February 18__ - MUIR, John A. and _____ [bride's
name omitted], by Russel B. Foster. (Dinwiddie County
D.B. 3, p. 609)

27 November 1850 - MUIR, William A. and Caroline F. Cousins, by
R. B. Foster. (Dinwiddie County Marriage Book 1849-1867
p. 102)

29 June 1793 - MUIR, Richard and Frances Liegh, King and Queen
County (Christ Church Parish Register, p. 116)

20 August 1789 - MUIRE, William and Catharine Seward, King and
Queen County. (Christ Church Parish Register, p. 267)

N

1 February 1816 - NACE, Wilson and Charlotte Ellison, both of
Hanover County. (Virginia Marriage Bonds, Richmond City,
by Anne Waller Reddy and Andrew Lewis Riffe IV, p. 21)

23 December 1822 - NAPIER, Thomas B. of Caroline County, and
Sarah Starke of Hanover County. (Rev. Talley's Register,
p. 1)

22 December 1852 - NEBLETT, Robert N. of Nottoway County, and

Mary Eliza Gilliam, eldest daughter of John W. Gilliam of Dinwiddie County, by Churchill J. Gibson. (Dinwiddie County Marriage Book 1849-1867, p. 110)

15 October 1845 - NELSON, Philip and Mrs. Jane E. Nelson, widow. (St. Martin's Parish Register, p. 30)

26 July 1844 - NELSON, Robt. Wm. and Miss Vir[a] (?) L. F. Nelson. (St. Martin's Parish Register, p. 30)

19 November 1777 - NELSON, Wm. and Milley Day. (Hanover County Licenses - marriage and ordinary. Date as reported by clerk)

13 da 10 mo 1678 - NEWBY, Nathan, son of William Newby of Nansemond County, and Elizabeth Hollowell, ye daughter of Alice Hollowell of Elizabeth River, married in her mother's house. (The Chuckatuck Friends Records, p. 127)

3 April 1782 - NEWCOMB, Bowden and Rachel Currie of King and Queen County. (Christ Church Parish Register, p. 269)

28 December 1761 - NEWSUM, Francis of Dinwiddie County, and Mary Simmons, daughter of Benjamin Simmons. Sur. and Wit. Richard Kello and Benjamin Simmons. (Marriages of Southampton County, Virginia 1750-1800, by Chapman and Knorr, p. 43)

13 September 1757 - NEWSUM, William of Dinwiddie County, and Elizabeth Gray, spinster, daughter of J. Gray. Sur. James Wall of Brunswick County. (Southampton County Marriage Register, p. 3)

17 October 1850 - NICHOLSON, Lewis C. and Ann E. Rowland, by J. M. Arnold. (Dinwiddie County Marriage Book 1849-1867, p. 101)

__ November 1776 - NICHOLSON, William and Lucy Chamberlayne. (James City County Licenses - marriage and ordinary. Date as reported by clerk)

27 December 1825 - NIXON, Thomas and Melinda Earnest, both of Hanover County (Rev. Talley's Register, p. 7)

__ September 1845 - NORRIS, James H. and Harriet S. McCaleb, by J. W. Roper. (Dinwiddie County D. B. 5, p. 391)

22 December 1787 - NORRIS, John and Agatha Garrett, King and Queen County. (Christ Church Parish Register, p. 266)

__ November 1777 - NUNN, Thos. and _____ [bride's name not shown]. (King and Queen County Licenses - marriage and ordinary. Date as reported by clerk)

21 February 1839 - NUNNALLY, Joseph and Julia Ann Parsons, by I. E. Hargrave. (Dinwiddie County D. B. 2, p. 529)

28 January 1839 - NUNNALLY, Obadiah and Sally H. Nunnally. (Dinwiddie County D. B. 2, p. 529)

1 December 1841 - NUNNELLY, Obadiah and Martha E. Parsons, by I. E. Hargrave. (Dinwiddie County D. B. 4, p. 407)

17 March 1834 - NUNNALLY, Samuel and Susanna Rawlings, by I. E. Hargrave. (Dinwiddie County D. B. 1, p. 195)

20 October 1777 - 20 October 1778 - NUTTALL, James Jr. and Ann Lewis. (Gloucester County Licenses, marriage and ordinary. Date as reported by clerk)

O

21 December 1866 - O'BRIAN, Pat and Miss Wash. (St. Martin's Parish Register, p. 33)

23 December 1787 - O'DEAR, David and Nancy Shepherd, King and Queen County. (Christ Church Parish Register, p. 266)

27 March 1783 - O'DEAR, Major and Rebecca Hooker, King and Queen County. (Christ Church Parish Register, p. 270)

10 September 1828 - OLIVER, Thomas and Miss Mary K. Lipscombe, both of Hanover County. (Rev. Talley's Register, p. 11)

14 January 1829 - O'NEAL, Thomas of King William County, and Miss Mary Garland. Sur. and Wit. Robert King. (Middlesex County Marriage Register, p. 100)

15 da 9 mo 1678 - OUDELANT, William of Chuckatuck, Nansemond County, and Christian Taberer, daughter of Thomas Taberer of Isle of Wight County. (The Chuckatuck Friends Records, p. 86)

P

29 December 1741 - PAGE, Mann, Esq. of Rosewell, Gloucester County, and Miss Alice Grymes, daughter of the Hon. John Grymes, Esq. Sur. and Wit. Robert Burwell. (Middlesex County Marriage Register, p. 1)

_____ - PAGE, John of Isle of Wight County and Felicia Hall, daughter of Moses Hall, late of Nansemond County, dec'd. (The Chuckatuck Friends Records, p. 154)

10 November 1847 - PAGE, John and Miss Elizabeth B. Nelson. (St. Martin's Parish Register, p. 32)

15 da 1 mo 1702 - PAGE, Thomas son of Thomas Page of Western Branch, Isle of Wight, and Isabell Lawrence, daughter of Henry Lawrence of Western Branch of County of Nansemond, married in house of Frances Denson, widow. Among witnesses: Thomas Page, Sr., brothers Michall Lawrence, Tho. Lawrence, and mother Alice Page. (The Chuckatuck Records, p. 139)

15 October 1840 - PARISH, James T. and Elizabeth A. Williamson, by I. E. Hargrave. (Dinwiddie County D. B. 3, p. 96)

26 May 1805 - PARKES, John and Agnes Holdsworth. Sur. John Holdsworth. (Charles City County Marriage License)

1783 - 1792 - PARKER, Robert and Mary Ann Whitlock. (Hanover County License - marriage and ordinary. Date as reported by clerk)

9 January 1777 - PARRISH, John and Sarah Wakefield. (Elizabeth

City County License - marriage and ordinary. Date as reported by clerk)

9 December 1834 - PARSLEY, John P., bachelor, and Miss Eleanor J. White, both of Hanover County. Married by Rev. Charles Talley 11 December 1834. (Hanover County Miscellany and Rev. Talley's Register, p. 21)

26 October 1840 - PARSLEY, William and Frances S. Atkinson of King William County. (Virginia Colonial Abstracts)

24 September 1835 - PARSONS, Henry and Mary Ann Parsons, by I. E. Hargrave. (Dinwiddie County D. B. 1, p. 373)

24 December 1830 - PARSONS, James of Hanover County and Elvira Wade of New Kent County. (Rev. Talley's Register, p. 14)

15 May 1834 - PARSONS, John and Ann E. F.Roggers, who consents. (Charles City County marriage licenses, box 9, V.S.L.)

12 August 1840 - PARSONS, Reynolds, bachelor, and Miss Coley Kerby. (Hanover County Miscellany)

4 June 1835 - PARSONS, Thomas T. and Mary Eveline Wells, by I. E. Hargrave. (Dinwiddie County D. B. 1, p. 373)

20 December 1848 - PARSONS, William and Virginia G. Williamson, by James D. Parker. (Dinwiddie County D. B. 6, p. 75)

17 November 1785 - PASLAY, Thomas and Winney Adcock, spinster. Sur. James Bristow. (Buckingham Marriage Bonds)

16 September 1788 - PATTERSON, Thomas and Elizabeth Dillard, King and Queen County. (Christ Church Parish Register, p. 194)

23 May 1826 - PATE, John and Maria Bowles, both of Hanover County. (Rev. Talley's Register, p. 8)

8 December 1824 - PEACE, Charles H. and Martha M. Turner, both of Hanover County. (Rev. Talley's Register, p. 4)

6 January 1825 - PEACE, William H. and Elizabeth Wade, both of Hanover County. (Rev. Talley's Register, p. 4)

3 December 1785 - PEARCE, Beverley and Tilly Webb, King and Queen County. (Christ Church Parish Register, p. 264)

13 December 1815 - PEGRAM, Benjamin of Dinwiddie County, and Catharine Ann Stith. Richard Stith of Brunswick County guardian of Catharine Ann and gives consent. Sur. and wit. John Fisher and Eliza A. Stith. (Greensville County Marriage Register, p. 76)

15 May 1855 - PEGRAM, Richard G. and Helen L. Burwell (Richmond). (St. Martin's Parish Register, p. 32)

12 March 1829 - PENDLETON, Hugh N. and Lucy Nelson. (St. Martin's Parish Register, p. 29)

8 May 1839 - PENDLETON, Hugh N. and Miss Elizabeth Digges (Louisa). (St. Martin's Parish Register, p. 30)

15 July 1831 - PENDLETON, William N. and Angolette E. Page.
(St. Martin's Parish Register, p. 29)

20 March 1850 - PERKINS, David and Elizabeth Abernathy, by
I. E. Hargrave. (Dinwiddie County Marriage Book 1849-1867,
p. 100)

4 February 1851 - PERKINS, Robert B. and Mary A. S. Wells, by
I. E. Hargrave. (Dinwiddie County Marriage Book 1849-1867,
p. 106)

3 September 1835 - PERKINS, Stephen F. and Miss Martha P.
Goode. (St. Martin's Parish Register, p. 30)

13 December 1849 - PERKINS, Thos. M. and Miss Evelina E. Mason.
(St. Martin's Parish Register, p. 32)

18 October 1848 - PERKINS, William S. and Mary E. A. Perkins,
by I. E. Hargrave. (Dinwiddie County, D.B. 6, p. 191)

16 November 1852 - PERKINS, William T. and Ann R. Major, by
J.W.M. Kirby. (Dinwiddie County Marriage Book 1849-1867,
p. 113)

__ December 1866 - PERKINS, Z.(?) and Miss Mallory. (St. Martin's Parish Register, p. 33)

25 July 1844 - PERKINSON, Jeremier and Elizabeth Clarke, by
J. W. Roper. (Dinwiddie County D.B. 5, p. 390)

20 March 1839 - PERKINSON, John W. and Elizabeth Stowe, by
W. Hyde. (Dinwiddie County D.B. 2, p. 329)

15 December 1836 - PERKINSON, William and Martha Stow, by
W. Hyde. (Dinwiddie County D.B. 1, p. 534)

29 September 1840 - PERRIN, Isaac Jr., bachelor, and Mrs. Jane
Kersey. (Hanover County Miscellany)

18 December 1833 - PERRIN, William K., Esq. of Gloucester
County, and Mrs. Sarah Tayloe Nicolson. Married 31 Decem-
ber 1833 by Jno. Cole of Gloucester County. Sur. and
Wit. Wyndham Kemp. (Middlesex Marriage Register, p. 113)

27 November 1783 - PERRY, Gregory and Mary Mills, Gloucester
County. (Christ Church Parish Register, p. 263)

7 February 1791 - PERRY, Littleberry and Lucy Gill. Sur. and
Wit. Stith Hardyman and Ro. Munford. (Charles City County
Marriage Licenses, Box 9, V.S.L.)

31 January 1852 - PETTUS, John J. and Eliza Hudson, by C. J.
Gibson. (Dinwiddie County Marriage Book 1849-1867, p. 107)

20 March 1849 - PETTUS, William H. and Mary E. Cox, by Russel
B. Foster. (Dinwiddie County Marriage Book 1849-1867,
p.102)

28 February 1787 - PHILBATES, John and Sarah Poynter, who consents. Sur. and Wit. John Evans and L. Bacon. (Charles
City County Marriage Licenses, Box 9, V.S.L.)

3 July 1777 - PHILLIPS, George and Ann Pettus. (Hanover

County Licenses - marriage and ordinary. Date as reported by clerk)   ·

19 January 1826 - PHILLIPS, George W. of Georgia, and Martha G. Skelton of Hanover County. (Rev. Talley's Register, p. 7)

[26] October 1784 - PHILLIPS, Henry and Frances Pearman. Consent only. (Charles City County Courthouse records)

6 January 1842 - PHILLIPS, Jno. W. and Jane R. Hitchcock, by I. E. Hargrave. (Dinwiddie County D. B. 4, p. 407)

23 July 1823 - PHILLIPS, Thomas and Judith Cocke, both of Hanover County. (Rev. Talley's Register, p. 1)

28 April 1818 - PHILLIPS, William, Jr. and Susanna Bickil. Sur. Edward Adams. (Charles City County Marriage Licenses)

13 November 1788 - PHILPOTS, John and Elizabeth McWilliams, Gloucester County. (Christ Church Parish Register, p. 194)

15 June 1793 - PICKET, Ashu and Mary Peerman who consents. Sur. John Pearman of Charles City County. Wit. Rebecca Pearman, Samuel Osslin, William _____, and Elizabeth _____. (Marriages of Henrico County, Virginia 1680-1808 by Joyce H. Lindsay, p. 66)

29 January 1782 - PIERCE, Thomas and Milly Webb of King and Queen County (Christ Church Parish Register, p. 261)

23 July 1845 - PILLION, Wiley and Dolly Minggee, by I. E. Hargrave. (Dinwiddie County D.B. 5, p. 59)

6 February 1793 - PINCHAM, Richard of Nottoway County, and Nancy Marshall, daughter of Mary Marshall. Sur. and wit. Joseph Moseley, William Moseley, and T. Turpin, Jr. (Powhatan County Marriage Register, p.24)

26 January 1837 - PINCHBECK, Robert and Mary E. Manlove, by Isham E. Hargrave. (Dinwiddie County D.B. 2, p. 37)

26 February 1849 - PINCHBECK, William J. and Antoinette Abernathy, by Edmund Withers. (Dinwiddie County D.B. 6, p. 119)

___ December 1776 - PITT, Wm. and Eleanor Weldon. (James City Licenses - marriage and ordinary. Date as reported by clerk)

10 da 1st mo 1765 - PLEASANTS, James, son of John and Susanna Pleasants of County of Henrico, and Dorothy Jordan, daughter of Pleasants and Mary Jodan, late of Nansemond County, dec'd. (White Oak Swamp Friends Records, p. 99)

10 da 11 mo 1768 - PLEASANTS, Joseph, son of John Pleasants of "Picquanocque" in Henrico County, and Elizabeth Jordan, daughter of Pleasants Jordan of Nansemond County, dec'd. (White Oak Swamp Friends Records, p. 158)

26 January 1793 - PLOOM, William and Sarah Woodcock, daughter of Susannah Jackson who consents. Sur. James Bullifant. (Charles City County Marriage Licenses, Box 9, V.S.L.)

20 October 1777 - 20 October 1778 - POINTER, Henry and Sarah
   Hall. (Gloucester County Licenses - marriage and ordinary.
   Date as reported by clerk)

21 July 1842 - POLAN, Benjamin F. and Malvina F. Crowder, by
   J. W. Roper. (Dinwiddie County D.B. 3, p. 565)

30 April 1838 - POLLAN, Thomas and Sarah A. Pollan, by J. W.
   Roper. (Dinwiddie County D.B. 2, p. 255)

19 November 1838 - POLLAN, Thomas N. and Mary Crowder, by J. W.
   Roper. (Dinwiddie County D.B. 2, p. 255)

10 January 1839 - POLLARD, Benjamin and Miss Camilla M. Price.
   (St. Martin's Parish Register, p. 30)

20 December 1831 - POLLARD, William T. H. and Susan C. Winston.
   (St. Martin's Parish Register, p. 29)

20 October 1777 - 20 October 1778 - POLLARD, William Jr. and
   Elizabeth Gressitt. (Gloucester County Licenses - marriage
   and ordinary. Date as reported by clerk)

15 September 183_ - POOL, Henry S. and Elizabeth M. Winfree,
   by W. Hyde. (Dinwiddie County D.B. 1, p. 417)

31 May 1849 - POOL, John W. P. and Susanna Moody, by I. E.
   Hargrave. (Dinwiddie County D.B. 6, p. 191)

11 da 2 mo 1708 - POPE, Wm. of Nansemond County and Mary Haile
   of Nansemond County. (The Chuckatuck Friends Records,
   p.147)

7 April 1841 - PORCH, James W. and Amanda G. Lewis, by I. E.
   Hargrave. (Dinwiddie County D.B. 3, p. 96)

17 December 1851 - POTTS, George W. and Mary E. Vaughan, by
   I. E. Hargrave. (Dinwiddie County Marriage Book 1849-
   1867, p.107)

1 February 1845 - POTTS, William B. and Charity S. Butler, by
   J. W. Roper. (Dinwiddie County D.B. 5, p. 391)

21 December 1848 - POWELL, Danl. L. and Miss Maria L. Temple.
   (St. Martin's Parish Register, p. 32)

26 November 1825 - POWERS, James of Gloucester County, and Miss
   Mary Bray, daughter of Thomas Bray. Sur. and wit. Enos
   Healy. (Middlesex Marriage Register, p. 93)

9 December 1841 - POYNOR, John and Martha Edwards, by T. T.
   Castleman. (Dinwiddie County D.B. 4, p. 126)

15 February 1794 - PRICE, James and Elizabeth Strong, spinster
   of full age. Sur. Johnson Strong. (Buckingham County
   Marriage Bonds)

27 November 1845 - PRICE, Maj. P. H. and Mrs. Mary B. Berkeley.
   (St. Martin's Parish Register, p. 30)

27 November 1757 - PRIDE, Hallcott of Dinwiddie County, and
   Mary Briggs, daughter of Capt. Howell Briggs. Sur. and
   wit. Henry Woodcock, Thomas Knox, and Gray Briges. (Sussex

County Marriage Register, p. 3)

20 December 1838 - PRITCHETT, Peter R. and Sarah Coleman, by
J. W. Roper. (Dinwiddie County D.B. 2, p. 255)

6 April 1836 - PRITCHETT, Richard F. and Mary Simmons, by J. G.
Claiborne. (Dinwiddie County D.B. 1, p. 391)

8 November 1840 - PROSISE, Samuel H. and Emily Ann Reames, by
Russel B. Foster. (Dinwiddie County D.B. 3, p. 609)

6 February 1833 - PROCISE, Thos. D. and Rebecca M. Rowland, by
I. E. Hargrave. (Dinwiddie County D.B. 1, p. 4)

2 December 1818 - PROSISE, William and Mariah Wells, by Chas.
Roper. (Dinwiddie County Marriage Book 1849-1867, p. 104)

20 October 1777 - 20 October 1778 - PROSSER, Jonathan and
Rachel Anthony. (Gloucester County Licenses - marriage and
ordinary. Date as reported by clerk)

5 December 1782 - PRYOR, John and Delphia Dillard of King and
Queen County. (Christ Church Parish Register, p. 262)

2 February 1824 - PRYOR, Samuel W. and Sarah Dudley Graves,
"first born daughter" of Edmond V. Graves and Betsy W.
Graves who give reluctant consent. Sur. Wm. S. Graves.
(Charles City County Courthouse records)

6 June 1835 - PURYEAR, John, bachelor, and Miss Mary S. Chester-
man, both of Hanover County. Married 15 June by Rev.
Talley. (Hanover County Miscellany and Rev. Talley's
Register, p. 22)

10 September 1842 - PYLE, John of Buckingham County, and Mary
Osgood, ward of Jacob Barnes. (Virginia Marriage Bonds,
Richmond City, by Anne Waller Reddy and Andrew Lewis Riffe
IV, p.78)

R

12 September 1840 - RABINEAU, George W. and Mary T. Meredith,
New Kent County. (Virginia Colonial Abstracts)

14 December 1780 - RADFORD, Wm. and Rebecca Winston. (Hanover
County Licenses - marriage and ordinary. Date as reported
by clerk)

3 May 1756 - RAINES, Frederick, son of Richard Raines of Prince
George County, and Frances Wyche, daughter of James Wyche,
dec'd. William Johnson, guardian of Frances. Sur. and
wit. Thomas Young, Isham Browder, Peter Jones, and Nathaniel
Raines. (Sussex County Marriage Register, p. 2)

7 May 1838 - RAINEY, Daniel E. and Martha J. Williams, by I. E.
Hargrave. (Dinwiddie County D.B. 2, p. 529)

13 June 1776 - RALLS, George and Jaine Dames. (Elizabeth City
Licenses - marriage and ordinary. Date as reported by
clerk)

20 October 1777-20 October 1778 - RANSONE, Thos. and Margaret
Gwyn. (Gloucester County Licenses - marriage and ordinary.

Date as reported by clerk)

17 da 3 mo 1802 - RATCLIFF, Isaac, son of William, dec'd of
    York County, and Margaret Crew, daughter of Benjamin Crew,
    dec'd of Charles City County. Married at Cedar Creek in
    County of Hanover. (Friends Records, Marriage Certificates
    1799-1808)

14 May 1840 - RATCLIFFE, Daniel, Esq. of Prince William County,
    and Mary Frances Bosher, daughter of James Bosher. (Vir-
    ginia Marriage Bonds, Richmond City, by Anne Waller Reddy
    and Andrew Lewis Riffe IV, p. 71)

16 September 1660 - RAWLISON, William and Jane Sparrow.
    (Charles City County Order Book, p. 270 and Virginia Colo-
    nial Abstracts, v. 11, p.92)

31 December 1846 - READE, Robert F. and Harriet B. Adams, by
    I. E. Hargrave. (Dinwiddie County D.B. 5, p. 295)

26 November 1846 - READE, William S. and Lucy Jane Adams, by
    I. E. Hargrave. (Dinwiddie County D.B. 5, p. 295)

1 February 1838 - REAMES, Albert H. and Martha H. Reames, by
    Russel B. Foster. (Dinwiddie County D. B. 2, p. 517)

29 December 1835 - REAMES, Green I. H. and Maria J. Crowder.
    (Dinwiddie County D.B. 1, p. 373)

6 October 1842 - REAMES, Winfield J. and Elizabeth D. Hoy, by
    J. W. Roper. (Dinwiddie County D.B. 3, p. 565)

8 October 1785 - REDDOCK, Collin of County of Hanover, Doctor
    of Medicine, and Jane Wyley Beverley, widow, of the County
    of King William. Sur. Richard Roy of Caroline County.
    (King William Record Book #2, pp. 69-73. Date is that of
    the marriage settlement)

8 February 1838 - REESE, Edwin J. H. and Henrietta B. Hawks,
    by Russel B. Foster. (Dinwiddie County D.B. 2, p. 517)

22 August 1850 - REESE, Herbert and Mary Ann Burnet, by J. W.
    Roper. (Dinwiddie County Marriage Book 1849-1867, p.105)

20 November 1839 - REESE, John and Mary A. F. Lamb, by Russel
    B. Foster. (Dinwiddie County D.B. 3, p. 609)

18 November 1839 - REMES, Stephen and Emeline Reames, by Russel
    B. Foster. (Dinwiddie County D.B. 3, p. 609)

29 March 1782 - RENINGHAM, William and Caty Kelligrew of Glou-
    cester County. (Christ Church Parish Register, p. 208)

10 October 1843 - RICE, Samuel T. K. and Mrs. Mary S. Ross, by
    C. J. Gibson. (Dinwiddie County D.B. 4, p. 674)

26 April 1849 - RICHARDS, Warren and Elizabeth Brown, daughter
    of Elizabeth Brown who consents. (People of color). Sur.
    Edmund C. Brown. (Charles City Marriage Licenses)

2 November 1840 - RICHARDSON, Henry C., bachelor, and Miss
    Elizabeth Melton. (Hanover County Miscellany)

19 February 1840 - RICHARDSON, John and Caroline Elder, by I. E.
    Hargrave. (Dinwiddie County D.B. 2, p.529)

21 December 1836 - RICHARDSON, John M. and Sarah Coleman, by
    J.W. Roper. (Dinwiddie County D.B. 2, p. 255)

25 December 1844 - RICHARDSON, Thomas W., bachelor, and Miss
    Polly Talley. (Hanover County Miscellany)

16 May 1839 - RICHARDSON, William E. and Harriet F. Pool, by
    James Morrison. (Dinwiddie County D.B. 2, p. 302)

28 February 1838 - RICHARDSON, William H., bachelor, and Miss
    Lucy Tate, both of Hanover County. (Rev. Talley's Register,
    p. 26)

20 October 1777-20 October 1778 - RICHESON, George and Mary
    Powers. (Gloucester County Licenses - marriage and ordi-
    nary. (Date as reported by clerk)

16 da 3 mo 1703 - RICKESIS, Abraham, son of Isaac Rickesis of
    the western branch of Nansemond River, and Mary Bellson,
    daughter of Edmond Bellson of Nansemond County. Wit.
    father, Isaac Rickesis; bros. John, Robart, and Jacob
    Rickesis; Uncell [sic], Wm. Scott, Sr. and Uncell Benjamin
    Small; mother, Kathren Rickesis; ante [sic] Elizabeth Small;
    ante, Mary Jordan. (The Chuckatuck Friends Records, p. 140)

1 January 1778 - RIDDICK, Constantine and MaryBizer. (Hanover
    County Licenses - marriage and ordinary. Date as reported
    by clerk)

__ May 1764 - RIDDLEHURST, John and Judith Miles, spinster.
    (Charles City County, William and Mary Quarterly, v. 8,
    p. 196)

22 December 1847 - RIDEOUT, Giles and Rebecca Jane Wells, by
    James D. Parker. (Dinwiddie County D.B. 6, p. 75)

28 January 1835 - RIVES, Robert C. and Ann Eliza King, by John
    Grammer, Jr. (Dinwiddie County D.B. 1, p. 244)

19 January 1775 - RIVES, William of Prince George County, and
    Jemima Heath, daughter of William Heath. Sur. and wit.
    Nathan Heath and Seth Heath. (Sussex County Marriage
    Register, p. 20)

27 November 1830 - RIVES, William and Dionysius R. Wells, by
    John Grammer, Jr. (Dinwiddie County D.B. 1, p. 244)

26 January 1787 - ROANE, Charles and Martha Garrett, King and
    Queen County. (Christ Church Parish Register, p. 265)

15 February 1754 - ROANE, William of Gloucester County, and
    Sarah Daniel, spinster. S ur. and Wit. William Upshaw of
    Essex County, W. Roane, Jr., and Thomas Price, Jr. (Mid-
    dlesex County Marriage Register, p. 8)

19 December 1850 - ROBERTS, John and Emaline F. Holliday, by
    I. E. Hargrave. (Dinwiddie County Marriage Book 1849-1867,
    p. 103)

20 October 1777-20 October 1778 - ROBERTS, Thomas and Ann

Burton. (Gloucester CountyLicenses, marriage and ordinary. Date as reported by clerk)

15 September 1852 - ROBERTSON, William H., Jr. and Elizabeth Rebecca Shore, by W. B. Tidball. (Dinwiddie County Marriage Book 1849-1867, p. 108)

8 March 1781 - ROBINNET, David and Patsey Anthony. (Hanover County Licenses - marriage and ordinary. Date as reported by clerk)

9 February 1788 - ROBINSON, Thomas and Elizabeth Dillard, King and Queen County. (Christ Church Parish Register, p. 266)

16 February 1837 - ROBINSON, William A. and Miss Elizabeth Peace, both of Hanover County. (Rev. Talley's Register, p. 24)

17 November 1835 - ROGERS, Daniel and Mary M. Jane Daniel, by Russel B. Foster. (Dinwiddie County D.B. 2, p. 517)

15 October 1698 - ROGERS, Francis and Apphya Miller. (Elizabeth City County, Deeds and Wills 1684,1688, and 1702, p. 168)

12 March 1848 - ROLLINS, Devereux and Mary A. E. Caudle, by J. W. Roper. (Dinwiddie County Marriage Book 1849-1867, p. 101)

8 February 1763 - ROOTES, Thomas Reade, of King and Queen County, and Martha Jaquelin Smith, daughter of John Smith, Esq. Sur. and wit. Augustine Smith of Gloucester. (Middlesex County Marriage Register, p. 14)

15 October 1850 - ROSE, Peter E. and Rebecca E. Rose, by J. M. Arnold. (Dinwiddie County Marriage Book 1849-1867, p. 101)

8 May 1845 - ROUNTREE, William and Miss Mary C. Blunt. (St. Martin's Parish Register, p. 30)

29 November 1804 - ROY, John Corrie of King and Queen County, and Elizabeth Corrie Williams. Consent by Beverley Roy father of the groom; and Catharine Williams, mother of the bride who states that Thaddeus Williams, father, is deceased. Wit. William Bird, Jr., Wiley Campbell of King and Queen County, and Kitty T. Roy. (Marriages of Richmond County, Virginia 1668-1853 by George H. S. King)

10 January 1820 - ROYALL, John, Jr. and Nancy Morgan. Sur. Wm. H. Gregory and Ro. W. Graves. (Charles City County. Certified copy of marriage license in John K. Martin papers, V.S.L.)

26 May 1785 - ROYALL, William Royall of Charles City County, and Susanna Hobson. Sur. Richard Povall. Wit. John Povall. (Powhatan County Marriage Register, p. 57)

22 November 1773 - ROYSTER, George and Anne Gergory, spinster. Sur. Wm. Gregory. (Charles City County Marriage Licenses, Box 9, V.S.L.)

26 October 1786 - ROYSTON, Thomas and Elizabeth Royston, Gloucester County. (Christ Church Parish Register, p. 265)

3 September 1813 - RUDD, James and Lucy Tinsley, daughter of
David and Ann Tinsley. Lucy born in Hanover 24 July 1792.
(Marriage Bonds from Records of Hustings Court, Richmond,
in Virginia Magazine of History and Biography, v. 34,
p. 170)

13 September 1781 - RUDOLPH, George and Elizabeth Hughes, Kingston Parish, Gloucester County. (Christ Church Parish
Register, p. 261)

24 May 1832 - RUFFIN, Wm. T. R., Esq. and Miss Ann M. D. Cocke,
by W. J. Plumer. (Dinwiddie County D.B. 1, p. 90)

19 April 1780 - RUSSELL, Richard of age 10 September 1779, ward
of Peter Williams of Prince George County, and Lucy Carter,
daughter of Joseph Carter. Sur. and wit. William Presley
Claiborne and William Horton. (Sussex County Marriage
Register, p. 26)

14 March 1785 - RYNER, Christian and Rhoda Dudley, Gloucester
County. (Christ Church Parish Register, p. 265)

S

20 November 1783 - SADLER, John and Mildred Corr, King and
Queen County. (Christ Church Parish Register, p. 263)

9 da 4 mo 1682 - SANDERS, William and Mary Hall of Nansemond
County. (The Chuckatuck Friends Records, p. 91)

11 October 1838 - SANDIFER, Turner and Mary A. Traylor, by
George A. Bain. (Dinwiddie County D.B. 2, p. 254)

1 December 1775 & 1 January 1778 - SANDRIDGE, John and Mary
Davidson. (Buckingham County Licenses - marriage and
ordinary. Date as reported by clerk)

20 October 1835 - SATCHFIELD, Isham B. and Lucy Ann Williams,
by I. E. Hargrave. (Dinwiddie County D.B. 1, p. 373)

28 September 1836 - SATCHFIELD, William and Mary Ann Jackson,
by Russel B. Foster. (Dinwiddie County D.B. 2, p. 517)

6 da 11 mo 1757 - SAUNDERS, Hezekiah, son of John Saunders of
Hanover County, and Martha Johnson, daughter of David
Johnson of Hanover. (White Oak Swamp Friends Records,
p. 14)

28 June 1787 - SAUNDERS, Nelson and Elizabeth Lewis, Gloucester
County. (Christ Church Parish Register, p. 193)

10 August 1848 - SAUNDERS, Stephen F. and Miss Betty L. Mallory.
(St. Martin's Parish Register, p. 32)

___ _____ 1777 - SCOTT, Anderson and ____ _____. (King and
Queen County Licenses - marriage and ordinary. Bride's name
not shown. Date as reported by clerk)

23 December 1845 - SCOTT, Berryman T. and Martha E. Brown, by
I. E. Hargrave. (Dinwiddie County D.B. 5, p. 59)

20 October 1777-20 October 1778 - SCOTT, Francis and Mary
Walker. (Gloucester County Licenses - marriage and

ordinary. Date as reported by clerk)

19 da 8 mo 1682 - SCOTT, Jno., son of William Scott of Chucka-
tuck in County of Nansemond, and Elizabeth Belson, daugh-
ter of Elizabeth Belson, married in her mother's house.
Among witnesses: father, William Scott, Elder; mother,
Elizabeth Belson; brothers, Edmond Belson, and William
Scott, Junr. (The Chuckatuck Friends Records, p. 64)

13 da 4 mo 1706 - SCOT, John, son of William Scot of Isle of
Wight County, and Joan, daughter of Thomas Took intend to
marry. "Joan is not of our Society." John disowned for
this action. (The Chuckatuck Records, p. 43)

17 January 1843 - SCOTT, Robert, Sr. and Sarah B. Thompson, by
Russel B. Foster. (Dinwiddie County D.B. 3, p. 609)

3 October 1835 - SCOTT, Simon and Sarah Ann Andrews, by W.
Hyde. (Dinwiddie County D.B. 1, p. 417)

28 da 6 mo 1707 - SCOTT, William, son of John Scott of Nansemond, dec'd, and Christian Jordan, daughter of Robert Jordan of Nansemond County. Wit. mother, Elizabeth Small;
Grandmother, Margaret Jordan. (Chuckatuck Friends Records,
p. 148)

18 September 1790 - SCOTT, William and Sarah Spruce. Sur. John
Carter who swears Sarah Spruce is above twenty-one years.
(Charles City County Courthouse records)

23 June 1802 - SEGAR, John and Ann Hillyard. Sur. Joseph
Hillyard and Nat'l Hillyard. Wits. Sally Edmondson, Mary
Hillyard, and James Hillyard. (King William County,
Book 4, p. 137)

24 September 1850 - SEWARD, James T. of King and Queen County,
and Frances E. Corr. Sur. and Wit. Thomas Corr and Perry
M. Peckham, Jr. (Middlesex Marriage Register, p. 139)

[no date shown] - SEYMORE, Edward and Mary More, by J. W.
Roper. (Dinwiddie County D.B. 5, p. 390)

27 April 1793 - SHACKELFORD, Francis and Mary Corr, King and
Queen County. (Christ Church Parish Register, p. 280)

14 February 1783 - SHACKELFORD, John and Mary Drummond of King
and Queen County. (Christ Church Parish Register, p. 262)

16 April 1791 - SHAW, William and Fanny Williams, King and
Queen County. (Christ Church Parish Register, p. 268)

14 December 1842 - SHELTON, Benjamin A., bachelor, and Mrs.
Eliza Burnett. (Hanover County Miscellany)

7 June 1849 - SHELTON, James B. and Miss Lucy C. Berkeley.
(St. Martin's Parish Register, p. 32)

7 January 1784 - SHELTON, John of Hanover County, and Anne
Southall. Sur. William DuVal. (Marriages of Henrico
County, Virginia 1680-1808 by Joyce H. Lindsay, p. 76)

21 January 1807 - SHIELDS, Matthew Wyatt and Mary R. Bell,
daughter of John Bell who consents. John B. Shields is

guardian of Matthew and gives his consent. Sur. Turner
Whit, and wit. Richard H. Bell. (Charles City County
Marriage License)

6 April 1842 - SHORE, John Dr. of Petersburg, and Martha P.
Branch, ward of William B. Giles. (Virginia Marriage Bonds,
Richmond City, by Anne Waller Reddy and Andrew Lewis Riffe
IV., p. 77)

1 November 1788 - SHORE, Thomas of Petersburg, and Sarah
Belsches. Sur. Hugh Belsches. Wit. Henry Shore. (Sussex
County Marriage Register, p. 52)

31 December 1776 - SIMPSON, William and Hannah Smith. (Elizabeth City County Licenses - marriage and ordinary. Date
as reported by clerk)

4 Xber 1697 - SKINER, John and Jane Smith. (Elizabeth City
Deeds and Wills 1684,1688, and 1702, p. 168)

28 September 1840 - SKINNER, Richard J. and Mary J. Lunsford,
by I. E. Hargrave. (Dinwiddie County D.B. 2, p. 96)

7 July 1773 - SKIPWITH, Henry and Ann Wayles, spinster. Sur.
James New and wit. Wm. Parrish, Jr. (Charles City County
Marriages)

7 June 1837 - SLATE, John W. and Elizabeth T. Roney, by Isham
E. Hargrave. (Dinwiddie County D.B. 2, p. 37)

6 December 1842 - SLAUGHTER, David S., bachelor, and Miss
Lucinda F. Gentry. (Hanover County Miscellany)

4 July 1849 - SLAUGHTER, George and Mary V. Moore, by J. W.
Roper. (Dinwiddie County Marriage Book 1849-1867, p. 102)

28 January 1778 - SLAUGHTER, John and Martha Kent. (Hanover
County Licenses - marriage and ordinary. Date as reported
by clerk)

2 June 1841 - SLAUGHTER, Thomas and Francis B. Lewis, by J. W.
Roper. (Dinwiddie County D. B. 3, p. 565)

12 da 1 mo 1699 - SMALL, Benjamin and Elizabeth Hollowell of
Nansemond County. (The Chuckatuck Friends Records, p. 131)

25 da 12 mo 1688 - SMALL, John, son of John Small of Nansemond
County, and Alice Holowell, daughter of Alice Hollowell of
Elizabeth River County, married in her mother's house.
(The Chuckatuck Friends Records, p. 126)

18 da 10 mo 1722 - SMALL, Joseph, son of John Small, and Ann
Owen, daughter of Gilbert Owen, both of Nansemond County.
(The Chuckatuck Friends Records, p. 157)

21 Oct. 1697 - SMELT, William and Eliza. Traverse, widow.
(Elizabeth City County, Deeds and Wills 1684, 1688, and
1702, p. 168)

8 November 1848 - SMITH, Albert T. and Martha P. Lee, by I. E.
Hargrave. (Dinwiddie County D.B. 6, p. 191)

19 November 1796 - SMITH, Edwin Bathurst of King William

County, and Sally Monroe. Consent of John Monroe, father of the bride. Sur. John Monroe. (<u>Marriages of Richmond County Virginia 1668-1853</u> by George H. S. King, p. 189)

14 November 1844 - SMITH, Edwin Harvie Dr., and Miss Anne G. Anderson, by C. J. Gibson. (Dinwiddie County D. B. 4, p. 674)

3 February 1778 - SMITH, Henry and Sarah Luck. (Hanover County Licenses - marriage and ordinary. Date as reported by clerk)

24 August 1836 - SMITH, Jeremiah M. and Miss Frances A. Chesterman, both of Hanover County. (Rev. Talley's Register, p. 24)

30 April 1776 - SMITH, Thomas of Hanover County, and Tabitha Williamson, daughter of Jacob Williamson. Sur. William Harrison. (Amelia County Marriage Register, S-1)

28 December 1826 - SMITH, John A. and Sarah H. Clayton. Sur. Edmund Christian. (Charles City Marriage Licenses)

26 March 1843 - SMITH, John S. and Paulina F. Doswell. (St. Martin's Parish Register, p. 30)

10 May 1860 - SMITH, Jonathan H., age 40, widower, and Mattie Tyler, age 24, single, daughter of William Tyler. The groom was born in Montgomery, Kentucky and his residence is given as Philadelphia. (Charles City County Marriage Licenses)

17 December 1829 - SMITH, Milo W. and Sarah T. Hall. (St. Martin's Parish Register, p. 29)

7 November 1799 - SMITH, Ned of Dinwiddie County, and Mary Huson, daughter of Ann Huson. Married by Rev. Stith Parham. Sur. Robert Nicholson. (Sussex County Marriage Register, p. 94)

13 March 1781 - SMITH, Thomas and Lucy Snead. (Hanover County Licenses - marriage and ordinary. Date as reported by clerk)

5 October 1848 - SMITH, William V. and Mary W. Thompson, by F. A. Gossee. (Dinwiddie County D.B. 6, p. 75)

22 May 1840 - SMITHSON, Green T. and Sally B. Davidson, by Jas. P. Owen. (Dinwiddie County D.B. 2, p. 610)

30 December 1824 - SNEAD, Dabney A. and Permelia Gentry of Hanover County. (Rev. Talley's Register, p. 4)

17 October 1858 - SNEAD, James H. and Martha T. Terrell. (St. Martin's Parish Register, p. 33)

27 December 1793 - SOUTHALL, Henry and Elizabeth Holdsworth, (Charles City County, <u>William and Mary Quarterly</u>, v. 8, p. 195)

18 December 1784 - SOUTHALL, John of James City County, and Susanna Sorsby. Sur. John Lucas, Junr. (Surry County Marriage Register, p. 14)

3 March 1780 - SOUTHALL, William and Sarah Dudley, spinster.
Sur. Mordecai Debnam and wit. James New. Note from John
Dudley to have his name on Mr. Southall's marriage bond.
(Charles City County Marriage Licenses)

22 December 1836 - SOUTHALL, Zattue W. and Elizabeth Davis, by
Russel B. Foster. (Dinwiddie County D.B. 2, p. 517)

2 September 1792 - SOUTHERN, John and Elizabeth Bowen, King and
Queen County. (Christ Church Parish Register, p. 280)

12 December 1850 - SPAIN, Albert E.and Susan P. Spain, by Hosea
Crowder. (Dinwiddie County Marriage Book 1849-1867, p. 102)

26 December 1833 - SPAIN, John B. and Nancy Reames, by W. Hyde.
(Dinwiddie County D.B. 1, p. 51)

6 March 1833 - SPAIN, Richard and Mary Ann Harmon, by I. E.
Hargrave. (Dinwiddie County D.B. 1, p. 4)

25 February 1836 - SPAIN, Robert H. and Louisa Starr, by I. E.
Hargrave. (Dinwiddie County D. B. 1, p. 373)

29 December 1792 - SPANN, Thomas and Patsey Hall, Gloucester
County. (Christ Church Parish Register, p. 280)

7 February 1799 - SPENCER, John and Molly Cooke of King and
Queen County. (Christ Church Parish Register, p. 336)

14 December 1693 - SPENCER, Thomas of King and Queen County,
and Elizabeth Whelling of this parish. (Christ Church
Parish Register, p. 62)

17 February 1787 - SPENCER, Thomas and Nancy Foster, King and
Queen County. (Christ Church Parish Register, p. 265)

24 December 1841 - SPIRES, Joseph and Nancy Wells, by Smith
Parham. (Dinwiddie County D.B. 3, p. 478)

21 May 1811 - SPROUSE, Rowland and Martha Gibson, daughter of
John Gibson of Buckingham County, "living in Chesterfield
with her sister Betsy Vest." Sur. John Vest. (Chesterfield County Marriage Register, p. 108)

4 da 6 mo 1758 - STANLEY, Archilaus, son of Joseph and Mary
Stanley of Hanover County, and Elizabeth Ladd, daughter of
John and Mary Ladd of Charles City County. (White Oak
Swamp Friends Records, p. 26)

4 da 12 mo 1757 - STANLEY, Pleasant, son of Thomas Stanley of
Hanover County, and Sarah McGee, daughter of Samuel McGee
of Hanover County, dec'd. Married at Wainoak Meeting House
in Charles City County. (White Oak Swamp Friends Records,
p. 15)

2 da 12 mo 1764 - STANLEY, Shadrack, son of John Stanley of
Hanover County, and Agness Ladd, daughter of James Ladd
of Charles City County. (White Oak Swamp Friends Records,
p. 98)

30 March 1852 - STANCIL, Samuel T. of Northampton County,
North Carolina, and Mary E. Darby of Dinwiddie County,
Virginia, by A. Stewart. (Dinwiddie County Marriage

Book 1849-1867, p. 108)

28 da 11 mo 1758 - STANDLY, William of Hanover County, and
Elizabeth Walker, daughter of William Walker, dec'd and
Sarah Walker of Loudoun County at Fairfax. (Fairfax
Monthly Meeting Marriage Records 1760-1892, p. 4)

6 da 3 mo 1775 - STANLEY, Zacheriah and Sarah Crew, married in
Charles City County. (White Oak Swamp Friends Records,
p. 228)

2 September 1790 - STARKE, John and Elizabeth Greyer. Wit.
George Brooks and Lucy Harris. (Hanover County Court Records 1783-1792. Date is that when the instrument was
recorded, not necessarily marriage date)

31 December 1823 - STARKE, Richard and Elizabeth Frances [sic],
both of Hanover County. (Rev. Talley's Register, p. 3)

15 September 1834 - STELL, Peter and Julia Ann Perkinson, by
I. E. Hargrave. (Dinwiddie County D.B. 1, p. 195)

20 December 1836 - STELL, Robert and Ann Browder, by J. W.
Roper. (Dinwiddie County D.B. 2, p. 255)

26 March 1833 - STELL, Shadrack and Eliza Perkinson, by I. E.
Hargrave. (Dinwiddie County D.B. 1, p. 4)

17 August 1833 - STELL, William and Martha Coleman, by R. B.
Foster. (Dinwiddie County D.B. 1, p. 298)

17 January 1782 - STEPHENS, John and Elizabeth Collier of
King and Queen County. (Christ Church Parish Register,
p.261)

10 October 1806 - STEWART, Armistead of Dinwiddie County, and
Flora Crook, daughter of Betsy Crook. Sur. Robert Crook.
(Brunswick County Marriage Register, p. 157)

26 January 1825 - STEWART, Daniel and Harriet Melton, both of
Hanover County. (Rev. Talley's Register, p. 5)

_____ _____ - STEWART, Edward R. and Tany R. Grant, free
people of color, by R. B. Foster. There was no date on
this marriage, but recorded 19 October 1835. (Dinwiddie
County, D. B. 1, p. 299)

3 November 1813 - STEWART, William and Ann Gary. Marriage contract recorded 28 February 1814. (King William County
Book 6, p. 307)

24 December 1833 - STEWART, William T. and Nancy Ruffin, by
W. Hyde. (Dinwiddie County D.B. 1, p. 51)

9 December 1783 - STONE, Job and Elizabeth Oakes, King and
Queen County. (Christ Church Parish Register, p. 263)

11 December 1850 - STONE, William A. and Mary J. Rose, by
James Jones. (Dinwiddie County Marriage Book 1849-1867,
p. 103)

8 October 1850 - STONE, William B. and Miss Mary P. Goodwyn, by
Jesse B. Spiers. (Dinwiddie County Marriage Book

1849-1867, p. 102)

18 October 1777 - STRACHEN (STRAUGHN), Alexander Glass Dr. of
Prince George County, and Lucy Pride. Colin Campbell of
Surry County guardian of Lucy. Sur. John Mason, Jr.
(Sussex County Marriage Register, p. 23)

7 April 1830 - STRACHAN, Alexander G. and Mary G. Boisseau, by
John Grammer, Jr. (Dinwiddie County D.B. 1, p. 244)

15 January 1784 - STUBBLEFIELD, Steth, and Lucy Timberlake
Southall. Edward Stubblefield consents to marriage of
Seth Stubblefield. Sur. Lud Southall and wit. Peter Royster. (Charles City County Marriage Licenses and Courthouse records)

22 January 1845 - STURDIVANT, Edwin and Sariah H. Rogers.
(Dinwiddie County D.B. 4, p. 768)

19 December 1833 - STURDIVANT, Henry and Lucy M. Hawkins, by
I. E. Hargrave. (Dinwiddie County D.B. 1, p. 195)

5 March 1840 - STURDIVANT, Henry and Jane Hawkins, by I. E.
Hargrave. (Dinwiddie County D.B. 2, p. 529)

4 February 1830 - STURDIVANT, Joseph and Mary Elliott, by John
Grammer, Jr. (Dinwiddie County D.B. 1, p. 244)

22 July 1841 - SUTTON, William M. and Miss Jane Eliza Doswell.
(St. Martin's Parish Register, p. 30)

22 December 1835 - SYDNOR, John T. and Elizabeth E. Meredith,
by Russel B. Foster. (Dinwiddie County D.B. 2, p. 517)

1 March 1837 - SYDNOR, Joseph and Mary U. Meredith, by J. W.
Roper. (Dinwiddie County D.B. 2, p. 255)

4 March 1778 - SYDNOR, William and Sarah Garland. (Hanover
County Licenses - marriage and ordinary. Date as reported
by clerk)

17 December 1833 - SYDNOR, William and Martha A. Young, by
R. B. Foster. (Dinwiddie County D.B. 1, p. 298)

12 May 1785 - SYKES, George and Alice Mourning Levingston,
King and Queen County. (Christ Church Parish Register,
p. 264)

28 January 1845 - TALIAFERRO, Lewis T., Dr., and Sarah C. Doswell. (St. Martin's Parish Register, p. 30)

4 January 1842 - TALLEY, Billy W., bachelor, and Mrs. Mary E.
Jones. (Hanover County Miscellany)

27 January 1846 - TALLEY, Billy W., widower, and Miss Mary
Elizabeth Pate. (Hanover County Miscellany)

19 December 1842 - TALLEY, Bowling, bachelor, and Miss Emily
Barker. (Hanover County Miscellany)

11 March 1840 - TALLEY, Hanswood, bachelor, and Miss Mary
Talley. (Hanover County Miscellany)

20 January 1847 - TALLEY, Henry, bachelor, and Miss Agnes Stewart. (HanoverCounty Miscellany)

26 January 1841 - TALLEY, James, bachelor, and Miss Elizabeth McDougle. (Hanover County Miscellany)

26 December 1833 - TALLEY, Nathaniel and Martha Gibson, both of Hanover County. (Rev. Talley's Register, p. 19)

7 June 1849 - TALLEY, Richard A. and Ann Eliza Ford, by J. W. Roper. (Dinwiddie County Marriage Book 1849-1867, p. 102)

18 August 1818 - TALLEY, Thomas and Nancy Eanes, by Chas. Roper. (Dinwiddie County Marriage Book 1849-1867, p. 104)

24 January 1829 - TALLEY, Thomas and Mary Turner, both of Hanover County. License obtained in Henrico County. (Rev. Talley's Register, p. 11)

30 August 1850 - TAPSCOTT, Benjamin G. of Buckingham County and Charlotte W. Wallace, daughter of William Wallace. (Virginia Marriage Bonds, Richmond City, by Anne Waller Reddy and Andrew Lewis Riffe IV, p. 107)

13 November 1833 - TATE, Francis, bachelor, and Elizabeth Kerbey, both of Hanover County. (Hanover County Miscellany and Rev. Talley's Register, p. 19)

1 August 1827 - TATE, John and Martha Melton, both of Hanover County. (Rev. Talley's Register, p. 9)

3 April 1823 - TATE, William and Miss Ann L. New. (Rev. Talley's Register, p. 1)

30 January 1773 - TATUM, Robert, son of Robert Tatum, deceased of Prince George County, and Amy Gee, daughter of Charles Gee. Sur. David Lessenberry. (Sussex County Marriage Reigster, p. 16)

1 November 1824 - TAYLOR, Francis and Elizabeth Shepherd. (St. Martin's Parish Register, p. 29)

16 December 1784 - TAYLOR, James and Nancy Wooton, of full age. Sur. Thomas Harris. (Buckingham County Marriage Bond)

13 October 1773 - TAYLOR, Richard of New Kent County, and Lucy Gregory, widow. Sur. and wit. James Eppes and James New. (Charles City County Marriage Register)

17 December 1807 - TAYLOR, William and Jane Morgan, daughter of Edward Morgan who consents. Sur. Benjamin Parker. (Charles City Courthouse records)

19 September 1811 - TAYLOR, William and Mary Lacy Vaughan, daughter of Henry Vaughan, who consents. Sur. and wit. John Wilson and Ro. W. Christian. (Charles City County Marriages)

3 August 1841 - TAYLOR, William and Jane Dickson, colored free. (St. Martin's Parish Register, p. 30)

__ January 1845 - TEMPLE, John and Rebecca Cross, by

J. W. Roper. (Dinwiddie County D.B. 5, p. 391)

22 September 1824 - TEMPLE, John S. and Maria D. Price. (St. Martin's Parish Register, p. 29)

18 November 1856 - TERRELL, Charles J. and Bettie T. Anderson. (St. Martin's Parish Register, p. 33)

15 da 4 mo 1804 - TERRELL, Joseph, son of Thomas Terrell of Caroline County, and Sarah Terrell, daughter of Jessee Terrell of said County. (Friends Records, Marriage Certificates 1799-1808, Cedar Creek)

24 April 1832 - TERRELL, Nicholas and Maria B. Doswell. (St. Martin's Parish Register, p. 30)

10 da 9 mo 1803 - TERRELL, Timothy, son of Thomas Terrell of Caroline County, and Mary Terrell, daughter of Pleasant Terrell of said County. (Friends Records, Marriage Certificates 1799-1808, Cedar Creek)

___ June 1786 - TERRY, _____ and Luch Lax. Sur. Elisha Lax. Record mutilated. (Buckingham County Marriage Bond)

19 December 1866 - THACKER, _____ Mr. and Miss Mallory. (St. Martin's Parish Register, p. 33)

18 March 1845 - THACKER, Henry and Elizabeth Ann K. Tucker, by I. E. Hargrave. (Dinwiddie County D.B. 5, p. 59)

10 July 1844 - THACKER, Milton and Emma A. G. Elyson, by J. W. Roper. (Dinwiddie County D.B. 5, p. 390)

7 November 1818 - THOMAS, Frederick and Agnes Valentine, by Chas. Roper. (Dinwiddie County Marriage Book 1849-67, p.104)

7 August 1758 - THOMAS, George of Hanover County, bachelor, and Dorothy Elliott, Henry Whiting, guardian of Dorothy. Sur. and wit. Henry Whiting, William Moulson, Mary Moulson, John Gordon, and Stanton Dudley. (Middlesex Marriage Register, p. 10)

27 January 1830 - THOMAS, John D. and Caroline E. Tyler, both of Hanover County. (Rev. Talley's Register, p. 12)

19 March 1835 - THOMAS, John D., widower, and Frances Ann Green, both of Hanover County. (Rev. Talley's Register, p. 22)

24 December 1783 - THOMAS, Mathew and Selah Holland, both of Nansemond County "and came over in absence of those who were licensed to marry in that county." Married by Rev. David Barrow. (Southampton County Marriage Register, p.637)

21 December 1825 - THOPSON [sic], James and Sarah Jones, both of New Kent County. This name is probably THOMPSON. (Rev. Talley's Register, p. 7)

30 May 1839 - THOMPSON, John Stith and Martha A. Crowder, by Russel B. Foster. (Dinwiddie County D.B. 3, p. 609)

15 April 1790 - THOMPSON, Robert and Lucy Barnes, who consents.
    Wit. L. Hardyman and Rach. Hardyman. (Charles City County
    Marriages, Box 9, V.S.L.)

31 August [1842] - THOMPSON, William F. and Mary Ellen Cousins,
    by Russel B. Foster. (Dinwiddie County D.B. 3, p. 609.
    The year of this marriage was not shown, but the list of
    marriages was recorded April 7, 1843)

2 September 1807 - THORNTON, Francis, Sr., of Gloucester County,
    and Miss Elizabeth L. Hackney. Sur. and wit. Benjamin
    Hackney and Francis Thornton, Jr. (Middlesex County
    Marriage Register, p. 64)

20 October 1777-20 October 1778 - THORNTON, John and Catherine
    Yates. (Gloucester County Licenses - marriage and ordinary.
    Date as reported by clerk)

5 September 1853 - THORNTON, Stuart G. of Fairfax County, and
    Margaret C. Glascock. (Virginia Marriage Bonds, Richmond
    City, by Anne Waller Reddy and Andrew Lewis Riffe, IV,
    p. 123)

9 January 1841 - THRIFT, Jacob S. and Arianna Evans, by Jos.
    W. D. Creath. (Dinwiddie County Marriage Book 1849-1867,
    p. 108)

11 December 1844 - THRIFT, Joseph B. and Ann T. Hawks, by I. E.
    Hargrave. (Dinwiddie County D.B. 5, p. 59)

6 September 1841 - THRIFT, William C. and Harriet J. Tucker,
    by T. T. Castleman. (Dinwiddie County D.B. 4, p. 126)

20 February 1851 - THRIFT, William T. and Ann C. Bristow, by
    I. E. Hargrave. (Dinwiddie County Marriage Book 1849-
    1867, p. 106)

20 October 1777-20 October 1778 - THROCKMORTON, John and
    Susanna Hughes. (Gloucester County Licenses - marriage and
    ordinary. Date as reported by clerk)

8 November 1827 - THRUSTON, John and Malvina D. Doswell. (St.
    Martin's Parish Register, p. 29)

1 December 1818 - THWEATT, Allen and Nancy M. Sutherland, by
    Chas. Roper. (Dinwiddie County Marriage Book 1849-67,
    p. 105)

19 December 1782 - THWEATT, David of Dinwiddie County, and
    Rebecca Gee, widow. Sur. Solomon Graves. (Sussex County
    Marriage Register, p. 31)

19 January 1830 - THWEATT, James M. and Elizabeth N. Rives,
    by John Grammer, Jr. (Dinwiddie County D. B. 1, p. 244)

7 November 1849 - THWEATT, William and Caroline Fraser, by
    Russel B. Foster. (Dinwiddie County Marriage Book 1849-
    1867, p. 102)

8 February 1842 - TIMBERLAKE, Benjamin A., Jr., bachelor, and
    Miss Elizabeth J. Archer. (Hanover County Miscellany)

30 January 1778 - TIMBERLAKE, Henry and Ann Austin. (Hanover

County Licenses - marriage and ordinary. Date as reported by clerk)

1 August 1840 - TIMBERLAKE, Henry, bachelor, and Miss Mary E. Tyler. (Hanover County Miscellany)

20 May 1788 - TIMBERLAKE, John and Susanna Christian, daughter of Gideon Christian, who consents. (Charles City County Marriages, and also in the courthouse records)

5 November 1823 - TIMBERLAKE, John E. and Margaret H. Colgin, who consents. Sur. Wm. B. Blaton. (Charles City County Marriages, box 9, V.S.L.)

7 September 1842 - TINSLEY, John W., bachelor, and Miss Eliza Martin. (Hanover County Miscellany)

18 April 1837 - TINSLEY, Philip M. and Miss Molly Ann Thomas, both of Hanover County. (Rev. Talley's Register, p. 25)

10 January 1833 - TOMKIES, Edward M. and Mary D. Christian. (St. Martin's Parish Register, p. 30)

29 December 1781 - TOWNLEY, Robert and Jane Anderson of King and Queen County. (Christ Church Parish Register, p.261)

15 June 1786 - TOWNSON, Joseph and Susannah Garrott, spinster. Sur. Stephen Garrott. (Buckingham County Marriage Bonds)

7 February 1840 - TRAYLOR, William, bachelor, and Miss Elizabeth Allison. (Hanover County Licenses - marriage and ordinary. Date as reported by clerk)

13 February 1783 - TRICE, Edward and Ann Jeffries of King and Queen County. (Christ Church Parish Register, p. 262)

30 March 1797 - TRIGG, John and Susanna Collier of Gloucester County. (Christ Church Parish Register, p. 302)

6 November 1832 - TROTTER, Isham A. and Louisa Watts, by Isham Eppes Hargrave. (Dinwiddie County D.B. 1, p. 4)

19 June 1787 - TROWER, Samuel and Allice Christian, daughter of Gideon Christian, who consents. Wit. Eaton Christian. Consent only. (Charles City County Marriage Register)

22 September 1831 - TRUEHEART, Peter G. and Elizabeth A. Frazer, both of Hanover County. (Rev. Talley's Register, p. 15)

6 January 1811 - TUCKER, Anderson of Dinwiddie County, and Nancy Abrams, 21 years of age. Sur. John Cordle. (Chesterfield County Marriage Register, p. 106)

17 May 1832 - TUCKER, Benjamin and Susan Tyler, both of Hanover County. License obtained in Henrico County. (Rev. Talley's Register, p. 17)

7 May 1834 - TUCKER, Bently and Miss Frances Hughes, both of Hanover County. (Rev. Talley's Register, p. 20)

13 May 1839 - TUCKER, Charles S., bachelor, of Richmond, and Miss Eliza B. White of Hanover County. Married 16 May

1839 by Rev. Talley. (Hanover County Miscellany and Rev. Talley's Register, p. 26)

January Court 1789 - TUCKER, David and Francis Jackson. Marriage Contract; proved by Nathaniel Eppes, Ralph Jackson and Daniel Tucker. (Dinwiddie County O.B. 1789-1791, p. 4)

13 December 1834 - TUCKER, Henry, bachelor, and Miss Sarah Barker, both of Hanover County. Married 17 December 1834 by Rev. Talley. (Hanover County Miscellany and Rev. Talley's Register, p. 21)

30 April 1831 - TUCKER, James and Sophia Davidson, both of Hanover County. (Rev. Talley's Register, p. 15)

8 March 1848 - TUCKER, James G. and Holly C. Tucker, by I. E. Hargrave. (Dinwiddie County D.B. 5, p. 578)

18 July 1782 - TUCKER, John and Frances Pigg, King and Queen County. (Christ Church Parish Register, p. 269)

___ December 1844 - TUCKER, John W. and Nancy Spain, by J. W. Roper. (Dinwiddie County D.B. 5, p. 390)

26 February 1779 - TUCKER, Joseph of Dinwiddie County, and Ann Sallard, daughter of Charles Sallard, who consents. Sur. Zachariah Hurt. (Amelia County Marriage Register, p.T-1)

6 May 1845 - TUCKER, Joseph, bachelor, and Miss Ann Wright. (Hanover County Miscellany)

14 December 1825 - TUCKER, Littleberry and Anne Talley, both of Hanover County. (Rev. Talley's Register, p. 6)

23 November 1835 - TUCKER, Richard G. and Mary E. Abernathy, by Smith Parham. (Dinwiddie County D.B. 1, p. 355)

2 September 1772 - TUCKER, Robert of Prince George County, and Mary Ann Parham. Sur. Stith Parham. (Sussex County Marriage Register, p. 16)

19 October 1825 - TUCKER, Stephen and Catharine Barker, both of Hanover County. (Rev. Talley's Register, p. 6)

24 December 1845 - TUCKER, Winfrey and Miss Elizabeth Barker. (Hanover County Miscellany)

17 June 1834 - TUNSTALL, Francis T. and Nancy Reames, by Pleasant Barns. (Dinwiddie County D.B. 1, p. 162)

4 November 1830 - TUNSTALL, Miles C. and Miss Eliza A. Burton, both of New Kent County. (Rev. Talley's Register, p. 13)

7 January 1795 - TUNSTALL, Robert of King and Queen County, and Ann Smith of Richmond County, daughter of John Smith who consents. Sur. and wit. David Williams, Fanny Smith, Patey Y. Richards, and Walter Burwell. (Marriages of Richmond County, Virginia 1668-1853, by George H. S. King, p. 219)

13 February 1778 - TURNER, Lewis and Agnes Turner. (Hanover County Licenses - marriage and ordinary. Date as reported by clerk)

14 October 1839 - TURNER, Thomas G., bachelor, and Miss Margaret
A. Via. (Hanover County Miscellany)

17 May 1827 - TYLER, James and Kitty Tombs, both of Hanover
County. (Rev. Talley's Register, p. 9)

24 December 1832 - TYLER, Littleberry and Catharine White, both
of Hanover County. (Rev. Talley's Register, p. 18)

14 March 1825 - TYLOR, Thomas and Lucy Lowery. (St. Martin's
Parish Register, p. 29)

1 January 1831 - TYLER, Thomas and Martha Ann Muller, both of
Hanover County. (Rev. Talley's Register, p. 14)

6 January 1836 - TYLER, Thomas, widower, and Miss Oney Via,
both of Hanover County. (Rev. Talley's Register, p. 23)

5 May 1812 - TYLER, Wat H. and Eliza W. W. Walker. Sur.
Sylvanus Gergory. (Charles City County Marriage Licenses)

9 July 1846 - TYLER, Wm. N. and Miss Malina F. Thompson. (St.
Martin's Parish Register, p. 32)

24 February 1831 - TYREE, Joseph and Martha Waddill, both of
Hanover County. (Rev. Talley's Register, p. 15)

18 November 1830 - TYREE, Wm. S. and Miss Ann M. Durham, both
of Hanover County. (Rev. Talley's Register, p. 14)

V

8 May 1849 - VADEN, John W. and Harriet P. Wells, by I. E.
Hargrave. (Dinwiddie County D.B. 6, p. 191)

9 April 1835 - VADEN, Page Harrison and Susanna C. Gunn, by
I. E. Hargrave. (Dinwiddie County D.B. 1, p. 373)

14 March 1842 - VAIDEN, Henry D. and Sarah M. Stubblefield,
daughter of J. S. Stubblefield. Sur. Robert W. Christian.
(Charles City County Marriage Licenses)

3 July 1828 - VAUGHAN, _____ of Gloucester County and Miss
_____ Wade of Hanover County. (Rev. Talley's Register,
p. 11)

12 December 1768 - VAUGH[N], William and Ann Dancy. John
Dancy consents. Consent only. (Charles City County
Marriages)

4 December 1834 - VAUGHAN, James W. and Martha Tally, by R. B.
Foster. (Dinwiddie County D.B. 1, p. 299)

21 December 1837 - VAUGHAN, James and Elizabeth J. Williamson,
by Isham E. Hargrave. (Dinwiddie County D.B. 2, p. 37)

4 December 1851 - VAUGHAN, Peter E. and Louise A. Michie, by
F. A. Gosee. (Dinwiddie County Marriage Book 1849-1867,
p. 106)

17 October 1850 - VAUGHAN, William and Mrs. Ann C. Brown, by
I. E. Hargrave. (Dinwiddie County Marriage Book 1849-1867,
p.103)

15 January 1844 - VAUGHAN, William H. and Ann E. Vaughan, by
   I. E. Hargrave. (Dinwiddie County D.B. 4, p. 407)

14 November 1832 - VIA, John and Miss Martha Parsley, both of
   Hanover County. (Rev. Talley's Register, p. 17)

22 February 1827 - VIA, Pleasant and Eliza Tyler, both of Hanover County. (Rev. Talley's Register, p. 9)

1 January 1825 - VIA, William and Martha Wicker, both of Hanover. (Rev. Talley's Register, p. 4)

                                W

2 February 1826 - WADE, Grandison of New Kent County, and
   Dicey Burnett of Hanover County. (Rev. Talley's Register,
   p. 7)

18 November 1830 - WADE, Granville and Lucy Higgins, both of
   New Kent County. (Rev. Talley's Register, p. 14)

30 August 1826 - WADE, John G. W. and Miss Elizabeth W. Talley,
   both of Hanover County. (Rev. Talley's Register, p. 8)

7 January 1830 - WADE, Robert and Ann Batkins, both of Hanover
   County. (Rev. Talley's Register, p. 12)

23 August 1829 - WADE, Thomas and Maria Gentry, both of Hanover
   County. (Rev. Talley's Register, p. 12)

16 January 1838 - WAIDE, Edmund of Hanover County, and Welthy
   Ann Atkinson of King William County. (Rev. Talley's Register, p. 25)

___ August 1785 - WAINWRIGHT, Samual and Nancy Thomas of Bath
   Parish, by Rev. Thomas Lundie. (Brunswick County Marriage
   Register, p. 345)

7 November 1849 - WAINWRIGHT, Samuel G. and Sally Eppes Spain,
   by I. E. Hargrave. (Dinwiddie County Marriage Book 1849-
   1867, p. 100)

29 January 1791 - WALDEN, Benjamin and Mary Dudley, King and
   Queen County. (Christ Church Parish Register, p. 268)

21 February 1793 - WALDEN, Benjamin and Mildred Didlake, King
   and Queen County. (Christ Church Parish Register, p. 280)

29 December 1791 - WALDEN, Charles and Mary Ison, King and
   Queen County. (Christ Church Parish Register, p. 197)

24 March 1792 - WALDEN, John and Frances Crittenden, King and
   Queen County. (Christ Church Parish Register, p. 257)

29 August 1789 - WALDEN, Lewis and Lucy Wallace, King and
   Queen County. (Christ Church Parish Register, p. 267)

25 October 1792 - WALDEN, Richard and Hannah Dudley, King and
   Queen County. (Christ Church Parish Register, p. 280)

27 October 1787 - WALDEN, Warner and Elizabeth Walden, King and
   Queen County. (Christ Church Parish Register, p. 193)

28 December 1795 - WALKER, Edward and Nancy Lo?[Lored ?] Sur.
Edward Davidson. (Charles City County Marriage Licenses)

1 December 1775-1 January 1778 - WALKER, Henry and Martha Jones,
(Buckingham County Licenses - marriage and ordinary. Date
as reported by clerk)

14 February 1855 - WALKER, Isaac Winston and Sarah C. Taliaferro. (St. Martin's Parish Register, p. 32)

20 June 1786 - WALKER, John and Mary Kidd, of full age. Sur.
Edward Herndon. (Buckingham County Marriage Bonds)

18 February 1796 - WALKER, Robert of Dinwiddie County, and
Mary Smith, daughter of Patience Smith. Sur. Newitt Drew.
Married by Rev. John Easter. (Sussex County Marriage
Register, p. 80)

21 October 1695 - WALKER, Thomas of York County and Eliza.
Johnson. (Elizabeth City County D. & W. 1684,1688, and
1702, p. 168)

4 February 1784 - WALKER, Wyatt and Elizabeth Christian, daughter of William Christian who consents. (Charles City
County Marriages, Box 9, V.S.L.)

24 March 1815 - WALLACE, Philip and Elvy Morriss, daughter of
James Morriss. Sur. James Morris. (Charles City County
Courthouse records)

26 December 1847 - WALLER, Benjamin and Sarah B. Moody, by
I. E. Hargrave. (Dinwiddie County D.B. 5, p. 578)

11 July 1695 - WALLER, James Mr., and Mrs. Ann Wythe. (Elizabeth City County D. & W. 1684,1688, and 1702, p. 168)

7 March 1799 - WALLER, John and Nancy Sears of Gloucester
County. (Christ Church Parish Register, p. 336)

15 December 1841 - WALTHALL, Christopher B. and Mary C. M.
Ford, by J. W. Roper. (Dinwiddie County D.B. 3, p. 565)

19 May 1852 - WARD, Robert F. and Louisa F. Shore, by W. B.
Tidball. (Dinwiddie County Marriage Book 1849-1867, p. 108)

8 November 1788 - WARE, John and Susannah Green, King and
Queen County. (Christ Church Parish Register, p. 194)

23 December 1823 - WARREN, George Washington and Elizabeth E.
Bailey. (Rev. Talley's Register, p. 2)

27 January 1848 - WARREN, James and Minerva J. Turner, by
W. O. Bailey. (Dinwiddie County D.B. 5, p. 493)

7 January 1826 - WAREN, Larkin and Sarah Martin, both of
Hanover County. (Rev. Talley's Register, p. 7)

9 May 1847 - WARREN, William W. and Mary J. Malone, by James L.
Gwaltney, Pastor of Baptist Church, Newville, Sussex
County. (Dinwiddie County D.B. 5, p. 500)

24 December 1846 - WASH, Wyatt and Miss Nancy Jane Lane. (St.
Martin's Parish Register, p. 32)

26 December 1833 - WATERS, James, widower of King William County, and Miss Judy Toombs of Hanover County. Married by Rev. Charles Talley. (Hanover County Miscellany and Rev. Talley's Register, p. 19)

4 February 1823 - WATERS, John of King William County and Jane Toombs of Hanover County. (Rev. Talley's Register, p. 1)

12 November 1777 - WATTERS, Nicholas and Sarah Rice. (Hanover County Licenses - marriage and ordinary. Date as reported by clerk)

2 September 1847 - WATKINS, James W. and Elizabeth E. Spain. (Dinwiddie County D.B. 5, p. 578)

21 December 1787 - WATTS, Edward and Ann Garrett, King and Queen County. (Christ Church Parish Register, p. 266)

22 October 1840 - WATTS, Josiah and Louisa F. Tucker. (Dinwiddie County D.B. 3, p. 96)

29 November 1842 - WATTS, Nathan M. and Ann W. Moore, by I. E. Hargrave. (Dinwiddie County D.B. 4, p. 407)

20 December 1832 - WATSON, George and Nancy T. Coleman, by W. Hyde. (Dinwiddie County D.B. 1, p. 51)

29 January 1683/4 - WATTS, Hugh and Joanna Marye in New Kent County. (Christ Church Parish Register, p. 22)

14 November 1818 - WELLS, Abraham V. and Sally Williams, by Chas. Roper. (Dinwiddie County Marriage Book 1849-1867, p. 104)

22 December 1836 - WELLS, Albert and Mariah Crowder, by W. Hyde. (Dinwiddie County D.B. 1, p. 534)

11 December 1818 - WELLS, Armistead and Dolly B. Williams, by Chas. Roper. (Dinwiddie County Marriage Book 1849-1867, p. 105)

27 March 1833 - WELLS, David and Mary Ann Connelly, by I. E. Hargrave. (Dinwiddie County D.B. 1, p. 4)

7 December 1840 - WELLS, Dickson and Nancy M. Wells, by I. E. Hargrave. (Dinwiddie County D.B. 3, p. 96)

16 December 1844 - WELLS, Drury and Louisa J. Hawkins, by I. E. Hargrave. (Dinwiddie County D.B. 5, p. 59)

28 December 1847 - WELLS, Francis and Sarah Jane Crowder, by Hosea C. Crowder. (Dinwiddie County D.B. 5, p. 500)

20 December 1842 - WELLS, Gilliam and Martha Hawkins, by I. E. Hargrave. (Dinwiddie County D.B. 4, p. 407)

20 December 1832 - WELLS, Green J. and Mrs. Martha J. Hawkins, by John Grammer, Jr. (Dinwiddie County D.B. 1, p. 244)

15 October 1834 - WELLS, Henry C. and Lucy Ann Vaughan, by I. E.Hargrave. (Dinwiddie County D.B. 1, p. 195)

24 December 1835 - WELLS, Henry V. and Nanny E. Grant, by I. E. Hargrave. (Dinwiddie County D.B. 1, p. 373)

8 September 1846 - WELLS, James A. and Lucy M. Alfriend, by I. E. Hargrave. (Dinwiddie County D.B. 5, p. 295)

11 October 1835 - WELLS, James B. and Wilmuth Ann Royal, by I. E. Hargrave. (Dinwiddie County D.B. 1, p. 373)

12 October 1849 - WELLS, James P. and Agnes Parsons, by I. E. Hargrave. (Dinwiddie County Marriage Book 1849-1867, p. 100)

24 December 1835 - WELLS, John C. and Louisa Nunnally, by I. E. Hargrave. (Dinwiddie County D.B. 1, p. 373)

28 January 1845 - WELLS, Laban and Matilda E. Andrews, by Hosea Crowder. (Dinwiddie County D.B. 5, p. 59)

30 December 1840 - WELLS, Stanfield and Mary Gilliam, by I. E. Hargrave. (Dinwiddie County D.B. 3, p. 96)

7 September 1843 - WELLS, Thomas and Ann A. Wells, by I. E. Hargrave. (Dinwiddie County D.B. 4, p. 407)

__ November 1785 - WELLS, William and Sarah Westmoreland of Bath Parish, by Rev. Thomas Lundie. (Brunswick County Marriage Register, p. 346)

16 January 1849 - WELLS, William B. and Mary E. Sturdivant, by I. E. Hargrave. (Dinwiddie County D.B. 6, p. 191)

16 October 1695 - WEST, Jno: Mr. of New Kent and Judah Armistead. (Elizabeth City D. & W. 1684,1688, and 1702, p. 168)

8 April 1786 - WEST, John and Rebecca Willcox, who consents. Wit. Ludwell Bacon. (Charles City County Marriage Licenses)

27 May 1820 - WEST, Thomas J. of Henrico, and Lucy Ann Randolph, daughter of Isham Randolph, who consents. Sur. Wm. Keesee. (Charles City County Marriage Licenses)

23 December 1824 - WEST, William and Susan Waddel, both of Hanover County. (Rev. Talley's Register, p. 4)

28 March 1814 - WESTMORELAND, Hartwell of Dinwiddie County, and Mary D. Branch, daughter ofEdward Branch. Sur. Archibald Hatcher. (Chesterfield County Marriage Register, p. 124)

13 April 1839 - WESTMORELAND, John R. and Sally A. B. Westmoreland, by I. E. Hargrave. (Dinwiddie County D.B. 2, p. 529)

20 June 1786 - WHEELER, James and Elizabeth Welch, spinster, of full age. Sur. John Welch. (Buckingham County Marriage Bonds)

12 December 1838 - WHEELHOUSE, Archibald H. and Dionetia Ford, by J. W. Roper. (Dinwiddie County D.B. 2, p. 255)

27 December 1843 - WHEELHOUSE, Henry L. and Lovely E. Ford,

by J. W. Roper. (Dinwiddie County D.B. 5, p. 390)

15 December 1852 - WHEELHOUSE, John B. and Julia Louise Virginia Clay, by H. B. Cowles. (Dinwiddie County Marriage Book 1849-1867, p. 109)

20 October 1777-20 October 1778 - WHITE, Edward and Pamela Singleton. (Gloucester County Licenses - marriage and ordinary. Date as reported by clerk).

7 November 1822 - WHITE, Josiah F. and Elizabeth Mileston, both of this county [Hanover]. (Rev. Talley's Register, p. 1)

23 July 1839 - WHITE, Samuel, bachelor, and Mrs. Ann W. Jones, both of Hanover County, married 25 July 1839. (Rev. Talley's Register, p. 26)

6 April 1831 - WHITING, John Randolph and Miss Louisa Beale by the Rev. Charles Talley, all of Hanover County. (Rev. Talley's Register, p. 15 and Richmond Enquirer, April 14, 1831)

9 November 1832 - WHITMORE, Charles H. and Lucy Ann Rives, by John Grammer, Jr. (Dinwiddie County D.B. 1, p. 244)

18 February 1836 - WHITMORE, George and Mary Ann Fraser, by Russel B. Foster. (Dinwiddie County D.B. 2, p. 517)

16 December 1850 - WHITMORE, George and Mary V. Wainwright, by R. B. Foster. (Dinwiddie County Marriage Book 1849-1867, p. 102)

25 June 1834 - WHITTACKER, Thomas E. and Mary E. Williamson, by I. E. Hargrave. (Dinwiddie County D.B. 1, p. 195)

1 June 1782 - WIATT, Pitman and Martha Fuller, King and Queen County. (Christ Church Parish Register, p. 269)

2 July 1785 - WIATT, Thomas and Catharine Robinson, Gloucester County. (Christ Church Parish Register, p. 264)

8 March 1847 - WICKER, Albert D., bachelor, and Miss Mary Peace. (Hanover County Miscellany)

19 April 1841 - WICKER, Bently, widower, and Mrs. Elizabeth Wright. (Hanover County Miscellany)

10 July 1832 - WICKER, Bentley and Martha A. Ellis, both of Hanover County. (Rev. Talley's Register, p. 17)

23 August 1837 - WICKER, James, widower, and Miss Maria Martin, both of Hanover County. (Rev. Talley's Register, p. 25)

12 May 1862 - WILEY, Oscar and Malvina Price. (St. Martin's Parish Register, p. 33)

24 December 1833 - WILKINSON, Joel M. and Elizabeth Grant, by R. B. Foster. (Dinwiddie County D.B. 1, p. 298)

15 May 1849 - WILKINSON, John S. and Minverva Hogwood, by C. J. Gibson. (Dinwiddie County Marriage Book 1849-1867, p. 103)

8 February 1808 - WILKINSON, Thomas and Nancy Bradley. Sur.
Seaton W. Crump and E. Christian. (Charles City County
Marriage Licenses)

21 da 9 mo 1723 - WILKINSON, William of Nansemond County, and
Rebecca Powel, daughter of William Powel of Isle of Wight
County. (The Chuckatuck Friends Records, p. 156)

23 January 1835 - WILLEROY, John, widower, of King William
County, and Miss Mary Jane Faulkner of Hanover County.
Married 24 January by Rev. Chalres Talley. (Rev. Talley's
Register, p. 22, and Hanover County Miscellany)

14 September 1848 - WILLIAMS, Adomiram and Syvelia Lumpkin,
daughter of Robert Lumpkin of King and Queen County.
(Virginia Marriage Bonds, Richmond City, by Anne Waller
Reddy and Andrew Lewis Riffe IV, p. 98)

20 November 1848 - WILLIAMS, Archer and Matilda Sandifer, by
J. W. Roper. (Dinwiddie County Marriage Book 1849-1867,
p. 101)

16 June 1762 - WILLIAMS, Boazure and Agatha Johnson, widow, who
gives her consent. Sur. and wit. Mordeccai Dednam and
Joseph Bishop. (Charles City County Marriage Licenses)

__1787 - WILLIAMS, Christopher and Aylie Snow, King and Queen
County. (Christ Church Parish Register, p. 193)

27 November 1845 - WILLIAMS, Herbert and Mary A. M. Browder, by
J. W.Roper. (Dinwiddie County D.B. 5, p. 391)

12 February 1850 - WILLIAMS, James W. and Arianne W. Jordan, by
J. W. Roper. (Dinwiddie County Marriage Book 1849-1867,
p. 105)

22 May 1844 - WILLIAMS, Joseph and Jane Haly, by J. W. Roper.
(Dinwiddie County D.B. 5, p. 390)

24 December 1844 - WILLIAMS, Joseph and Ann Caudle, by I. E.
Hargrave. (Dinwiddie County D.B. 5, p. 59)

20 December 1848 - WILLIAMS, Leroy A. and Lucy T. Moody, by
I. E. Hargrave. (Dinwiddie County D.B. 6, p. 191)

26 September 1847 - WILLIAMS, Newman and Martha Thweatt, by
I. E. Hargrave. (Dinwiddie County D.B. 5, p. 578)

22 December 1835 - WILLIAMS, Numan and Winsy J. Wells, by
I. E. Hargrave. (Dinwiddie County D.B. 1, p. 373)

5 November 1818 - WILLIAMS, Robert and Mary Caudle, by Chas.
Roper. (Dinwiddie County Marriage Book 1849 - 1867, p. 104)

18 April 1844 - WILLIAMSON, Edward and Margaret Williams, by
J. W.Roper. (Dinwiddie County D.B. 5, p. 390)

16 October 1838 - WILLIAMSON, Francis M. and Susan E. Heath, by
I. E. Hargrave. (Dinwiddie County D.B. 2, p. 529)

18 December 1818 - WILLIAMSON, Isaac and Catharine Wells, by
Chas. Roper. (Dinwiddie County Marriage Book 1849-1867,
p. 105)

12 January 1850 - WILLIAMSON, Robert A. and Matilda Caudle, by
   J. W. Roper. (Dinwiddie County Marriage Book 1849-1867,
   p. 102)

1 February 1836 - WILLIAMSON, William and Miss Elizabeth C.
   DeJarnette. (St. Martin's Parish Register, p. 30)

20 October 1812 - WILLIS, Samuel and Hetty Foset, who consents.
   Sur. and wit. William Cardwell and Ro. W. Christian.
   (Charles City County Marriage Licenses)

26 September 1838 - WILLS, Thomas B. and Mary G. Fisher, by
   Russel B. Foster. (Dinwiddie County D.B. 2, p. 517)

16 September 1698 - WILSON, William and Jane Davis. (Elizabeth
   City D. & W. 1684,1688, and 1702, p. 168)

12 January 1864 - WINE, Charles W. and Mrs. Frances E. Butler.
   (St. Martin's Parish Register, p. 33)

30 August 1838 - WINFIELD, Jefferson and Martha Ann Scott, free
   people of color, by W. Hyde. (Dinwiddie County D.B. 2,
   p. 329)

__ September 1845 - WINFREE, George N. and Mary Jane E. Hargrave, by Jno. Early. (Dinwiddie County MarriageFile
   1909-1913)

14 March 1810 - WINFREY, Henry and Sally P. Totty who writes
   her own consent. Sur. Chas. A. Cousins. Henry Winfrey
   qualified as guardian for Sally P. Totty, orphan of William
   Totty, dec'd at Dinwiddie Court House. (Amelia County
   Marriage Register, p. W-5b)

1 February 1781 - WINGFIELD, John and Rebecca Nelson. (Hanover
   County Licenses - marriage and ordinary. Date as reported
   by clerk)

1 December 1775-1 January 1778 - WINSTON, Anthony, Junr. and
   Keziah Jones. (Buckingham County Licenses - marriage and
   ordinary. Date as reported by clerk)

1 December 1825 - WINSTON, Edmund and Sarah Ann Terril. (St.
   Martin's Parish Register, p. 29)

30 March 1829 - WINSTON, Philip B. and Jane D. Price. (St.
   Martin's Parish Register, p. 29)

7 October 1856 - WINSTON, William D., Jr. and Margaret A.
   Vaughan. (St. Martin's Parish Register, p. 33)

__ December 1827 - WISDOM, Tavener of Spottsylvania County and
   Ynity Jones Hooper of Hanover. (Rev. Talley's Register,
   p. 10)

30 January 1845 - WOOD, Daniel, bachelor, and Miss Margaret E.
   Burnett. (Hanover County Miscellany)

30 November 1840 - WOOD, David, bachelor, and Miss Martha E.
   Burnett. (hanover County Miscellany)

25 April 1825 - WOOD, Henry T. and Catharine P. White. (Rev.
   Talley's Register, p. 5)

23 December 1844 - WOOD, James and Sally E. Pillion, by I. E. Hargrave. (Dinwiddie County D.B. 5, p. 59)

1 April 1825 - WOOD, John and Mary M. Martin. (St. Martin's Parish Register, p. 29)

28 November 1849 - WOODCOCK, Henry and Mary A. Blanks, daughter of Miles Blanks, deceased. Sur. Nathaniel Penny. (Charles City County Marriage Licenses)

12 June 1769 - WOODRUFFE, Job and Mary Clarke. Benjamin Cocke, guardian, gives consent. (Virginia Magazine of History and Biography, v. 23, p. 86)

7 da 1 mo 1768 - WOODSON, Charles, Jr., son of Charles Woodson of Henrico County, and Ann Trotter, daughter of Thomas Trotter of Nansemond County, dec'd. (White Oak Swamp Friends Records, p. 145)

11 September 1806 - WOODSON, George and Delphia White, who consents. Sur. and wit. Benjamin Thomas and Edm'd Christian. (Charles City County Marriage Licenses)

30 January 1844 - WOODDY, Arthur Q., bachelor, and Miss Martha Ellen Thomas. (Hanover County Miscellany)

30 January 1844 - WOODDY, Augustine D., bachelor, and Miss Mary E. Bootwright. (Hanover County Miscellany)

19 December 1833 - WOODDY, William H. and Sarah A. Thomas, both of Hanover County. License obtained in Henrico County. (R-v. Talley's Register, p. 19)

14 August 1684 - WOODWARD, William of Ware River and Bridget Williams of this Parish. (Christ Church Parish Register, p. 23)

16 February 1687 - WORMELEY, Ralph Esq. and Madam Elizabeth Armisted of Gloucester. (Christ Church Parish Register, p. 36)

29 November 1832 - WORSHAM, George and Marth Ann Wynn, by I. E. Hargrave. (Dinwiddie County D.B. 1, p. 4)

31 January 1780 - WORSLEY, John and Susanna Thompson. (Hanover County Licenses - marriage and ordinary. Date as reported by clerk)

11 May 1826 - WRIGHT, David and Elizabeth Martin, both of Hanover County. (Rev. Talley's Register, p. 8)

19 November 1836 - WRIGHT, David, widower, and Sarer Martin, both of Hanover County. (Rev. Talley's Register, p. 24)

16 May 1840 - WRIGHT, Fayette, bachelor, and Miss Mary Johnson. (Hanover County Miscellany)

7 June 1786 - WRIGHT, John of Hanover County, and Ann Puryear, daughter of Margaret Puryear who consents. Sur. and wit. Ruben Puryear, John Bowles, and Jesse Puryear. (Marriages of Henrico County, Virginia 1680-1808 by Joyce A. Lindsay, p. 96)

3 August 1828 - WRIGHT, John and Mrs. Catharine Tucker, both of
Hanover County. (Rev. Talley's Register, p. 11)

28 February 1829 - WRIGHT, John and Agness Melton, both of
Hanover County. (Rev. Talley's Register, p. 11)

1 November 1784 - WRIGHT, Stephen and Peggy Brooks, spinster
of full age. Sur. Peter Ford. (Buckingham County Marriage Bonds)

23 December 1781 - WRIGHT, William and Martha Jackson, spinster.
(Charles City County, William and Mary Quarterly, p. 193)

30 March 1783 - WRIGHT, William and Mary Bowers, King and
Queen County. (Christ Church Parish Register, p. 270)

23 July 1767 - WYATT, Hubbard and Tabitha Minge, daughter of
George Minge who consents. Consent only. (Charles City
County Marriage Register)

31 December 1805 - WYATT, Hubbard, Jr. of Dinwiddie County, and
Betsy S. Avery, daughter of Billy H. Avery of Prince George
County, now deceased. Sur. and Wit. Robert Greenway.
(Greenville County Marriage Register, p. 57)

2 October 1790 - WYATT, Peter and Joice [or Josie] Shepherd,
King and Queen County. (Christ Church Parish Register,
p. 268)

21 December 1836 - WYNN, Archer P. and Barsena L. Gunn, by
Isham E. Hargrave. (Dinwiddie County D.B. 2, p. 37)

Y

1 February 1826 - YARBROUGH, Jesse and Anne Bowe, both of
Hanover County. (Rev. Talley's Register, p. 7)

20 October 1777-20 October 1778 - YATES, Robert and Mary
Tomkies. (Gloucester County Licenses - marriage and
ordinary. Date as reported by clerk)

24 March 1831 - YEAMANS, Pleasant and Mary Walton. (St.
Martin's Parish Register, p. 29)

28 November 1839 - YOUNG, Benjamin H. and Martha A. Young,
by I. E. Hargrave. (Dinwiddie County D.B. 2, p. 529)

26 December 1837 - YOUNG, Charles and Lucy J. Eanes, by Russel
B. Foster. (Dinwiddie County D.B. 2, p. 517)

22 September 1852 - YOUNG, Charles W. U. and Lucy V. A. Foster,
by A. Stewart. (Dinwiddie County Marriage Book 1849-
1867, p. 108)

21 August 1815 - YOUNG, Edward and Jernelle Stell [or Stall].
Sur. John Creighton. (Charles City County Marriage
Register)

31 January 1838 - YOUNG, Francis and Mary M. Perkins, by
Isham E. Hargrave. (Dinwiddie County D.B. 2, p. 37)

___ October 1775 - YOUNG, Hugh and Mary Selden. (Elizabeth
City County Licenses - marriage and ordinary. Date as

reported by clerk)

5 September 1849 - YOUNG, John F. and Martha J. Wilson, by
   J. M. Arnold.   (Dinwiddie County Marriage Book 1849-
   1867, p. 100)

16 March 1841 - YOUNG, Joseph H. and Miss Ann Eliza Thompson.
   (St. Martin's Parish, p. 30)

26 June 1850 - ZEHMER, Charles G. and Miss Jane Manlove Bourdon,
   by Wellington E. Webb.   (Dinwiddie County Marriage Book
   1849-1867, p. 100)

Brides', Sureties', and Other Names

www.ingramcontent.com/pod-product-compliance
Lightning Source LLC
Chambersburg PA
CBHW021837020426
42334CB00014B/663